ABOUT THE AUTHOR

Clare Wignall has the good fortune to live with a sweet-natured family of a husband and two daughters who have been happy to taste test her fusion kitchen experiments, created whenever the money was tight. Multiculturalism and veganism are her twin passions. Having held a variety of jobs, from teaching in a secondary school to working with refugees, she has been privileged to observe over the years how diverse people combine culinary creativity with a limited income.

CLARE WIGNALL

Frugal Fusion Foods

AUSTIN MACAULEY PUBLISHERS™

LONDON • CAMBRIDGE • NEW YORK • SHARJAH

A CIP catalogue record for this title is available from the British Library.

ISBN 9781398401402 (Paperback)
ISBN 9781398400993 (ePub e-book)

www.austinmacauley.com

First Published 2024
Austin Macauley Publishers Ltd®
1 Canada Square
Canary Wharf
London
E14 5AA

DEDICATION

I dedicate this book to Peter, Octavia and Bathsheba, with all my love and thanks.

ACKNOWLEDGEMENTS

I would like to thank Jason Dodd for his masterly photography and monumental patience. I also want to convey my happy gratitude to Abi Hill for her beautiful and imaginative artwork, and for always being able to convey what I wanted to say. I am similarly greatly indebted to Karen Nugent for all her support, gorgeous sewing and ideas for the layouts of the High Teas.

Finally, I would like to express my sincerest appreciation to all the people at Austin Macauley Publishers for their encouragement, work and expertise.

CONTENTS

Introduction

What is "Frugal Fusion" Food?

Fusion, the "process or result of joining two or more things together to form a single entity" is magical! So, if we're talking about food, this means mixing together two cuisines (or more) to create a new dish. Freed from what is 'right' or 'wrong' in a recipe, you can blend cuisines and conjure, like the imaginative person you are, your own dish.

Blending cuisines dates from when we started migrating; most of the food we eat now has its origins in more than one country and recipes are being created and developed all the time, making our culinary choices all the more diverse and rich because of it. We now have the most glorious, multiple-textured, flavour-popping iconic dishes like Californian Sushi, Nan Bread Pizza, Korean Tacos, Peruvian/Italian Green Noodles and international, infinite varieties of curry, along with the daily concoctions being created by improvising cooks everywhere. What follows are my own fusion recipes or fusion classics I've tweaked to ease them into our frugal budget.

"Frugal Fusion" is the phrase I have given to describe this tweaking which goes on all the time with 'traditional' recipes which allows us to play with our food, by adapting recipes to fit what we can afford. Sometimes following a thoroughbred recipe can be terribly expensive when the ingredients used have to be bought online because we can't get them where we live.

I say this without any disrespect to the countries in which the dishes originated. On the contrary; often blending two or more cultures is the only way we can afford a taste indicative of a particular cuisine we want to try later when funds allow. Even more positively, sometimes that blending can bring out the best of both worlds. That is one of the pleasures of multiculturalism, culinary or otherwise: we can continually learn from each other and choose what works optimally for everyone. The result in this case is big tastes; if you want them on a small budget, you've picked up the right book.

You've also made the right choice if you need a little breather from teasing out the most efficient way of providing delicious inexpensive food, because everything has been worked out for you: menu planning for three meals a day, calculations, time effective food preparation, shopping lists, the using up of ingredients, the inclusion of (at least) your five-a-day and the stocking of the store cupboard. No one is suggesting you're too daft to do this yourself, of course, but if you lead a very full life, you may welcome relinquishing a little headspace now and then. During busy times of my own when fatigue was hitting, I would often think, *"Wouldn't it be great if someone worked out the week's meals for me, and the money as well, without assuming I have a mystical, magically self-stocking store cupboard?"* It is often said it is a good thing to write the book you wish had been written, so I have done just that, with the sincere hope that it will be helpful to you.

Why Plant Based?

I do not wish animals to be killed/exploited on my behalf, which is why I went vegan, but whether you are vegan or not, if you follow these plans you can be free of the worry that you are getting enough fruits and veggies on a limited budget, and you will see that plant food need not be expensive. It is vibrant, varied, fresh and a lot of fun.

Veganism lends itself beautifully to fusion cooking (or is it the other way around?) because delicious plant-based meals often borrow freely from other cultures, giving us the happy, humane choice of many recipes which have always been vegan (like Hummus, Aloo Gobi, types of Meze, Guacamole, Vegetable Tempura, varieties of bread like Puri or Pitta Bread, Patatas Bravas, Miso or Minestrone Soup, to name a tiny few) which we can adapt to fit our leftovers, meal and/or pocket. Additionally, we can easily veganise iconic fusion classics like Spaghetti with Meatballs, Tex Mex delights or Pissaladiere Pizza.

How This Book Works

This book is as honest as possible about how much your food bill will come to; there won't be any mention of how much something costs per portion, because you cannot buy half a block of tofu or a quarter of an onion. Instead, I have worked out a budget plan of weekly seasonal menus for around £65 or under for three meals a day for four people, including anything that may need to be bought for the store cupboard. Of course, prices vary constantly, and new lines are being added/discontinued all the time, but that is the ballpark figure; please see below. The essential point is that you don't have to keep buying things because the budget and the stocking of the store cupboard have already been calculated. Store cupboards are replenished not by magic, nor are fridges or freezers, but by our wallets, so I was very strict with myself in giving you an accurate representation of the real cost of the menus. If any of the items in recipes are already stocked in your home, you'll be able to shave off more from your expenditure, but I haven't assumed anything; everything has to be bought at some point, after all, whether it is tinned tomatoes, onions, garlic, oil, vanilla essence, stock cubes or any other item often regarded as a "basic" store cupboard ingredient. I haven't included salt, unless a specific type was needed for a recipe, but there is wriggle room within the budgets. (At the time of writing, you can buy 750g table salt for as little as 27p (Aldi); my personal preference would be to buy 500g of sea salt for 99p from Holland and Barret, which will last for at least a year).

The weekly budget includes detailed recipes for dinner (or, in other words, your main meal for the day) and suggestions for lunch and breakfast. Each week comes with its own shopping list for dinners and another for breakfasts/lunches. Just to reiterate, I have allowed for each ingredient: if a recipe calls for soy sauce, I have factored it in and not blithely presumed you have it in the cupboard already. To keep within budget and to stock the store cupboard at the same time, the plan works on three-weekly cycles. For example, if you have bought said soy sauce in the first week and need it in the second, it will have already been bought and will not appear in the second week's shopping list. Using this method, I was able to stick within the budget. However, if you do not wish to be committed to the three weeks, at the end of each shopping list it says what has already been accounted for, so you can see what you may need if you haven't been following the cycle.

About the Breakfasts and Lunches

The breakfasts and lunches have their own shopping lists but also call upon ingredients bought for the dinners and/or previous lunches/breakfasts in the cycle. That way, not only will you be in a position to stick within the budget, you'll also be able to use all the potatoes or finish up the bag of rice. These lists also work within the three-week cycle principle so if, for example, you bought a 1kg bag of rice, it could well be dipped into for a dinner one week and a lunch the next. Again, if this sounds too restrictive, every list of suggestions for breakfasts and lunches finishes with what has already been factored in, so you can tell at a glance if you need to buy anything if you are picking ideas at random. All becomes clear when you look at the lists!

The breakfasts and lunches are, on the whole, simple because not everyone has the time to make three complex meals a day. There are a few special treats here and there, however. I haven't included a recipe for porridge or overnight oats as the ratio of oats-to-liquid which people prefer varies; my prefer-ence is a 2 part liquid to 1 part oat ratio for both recipes. The latter recipe is obviously oats (with additions or later toppings) soaked overnight; the former, I find, takes just a few minutes to thicken up on the hob. I allow about 50g oats to 240ml liquid per person (½ American cup to 1 American cup). I use water to keep within the budget (and oats are naturally creamy) but if this is too austere for you, plant milk is great if you want to stray just a little outside the allowance; there will be some milk left anyway if you don't drink tea by the gallon like me.

I have tended to provide notes about the lunches as their titles are fairly self-explanatory; however, when the instructions are more complicated, I have provided recipes. When I call a wrap a "burrito" it just means beans are included in the filling, although, as you would expect, all of them wander outside the parameters of Mexican cuisine! When I call a recipe a "taco" the idea is that the shell encasing the filling is smaller, and more firm; so if you wish, you can either grill, bake or lightly fry your wrap. Finally, in case you've never had the pleasure, a taquito is a tortilla wrap rolled up into a cigar shape; in other words, it's a "little taco".

High Teas

When you are juggling limited funds, especially for some time, you stand more chance of keeping the balls in the air if you have fun varying your juggling patterns. For this reason I have worked four themed High Teas into the budgets; one for every season, each embracing the spiral pattern. Naturally, you may want to use your own ideas or shapes instead, but these promise to stay within the designated figure.

Can Smaller Households Use this Book?

You can still use this book if you're not part of a household of four. If there are two of you, you can simply halve the quantities used in the recipes. A good set of measuring spoons is useful to have in this case, as the smallest spoon is 1/8th of a teaspoon. (You can buy a set for as little as £2.80 on Amazon at the time of writing). You would then have to halve the number of fruits/veggies on the shopping list, and put any half packets of vegan cheese/tofu in airtight boxes to be used later (tweaking the lunch shopping list, perhaps, and using these ingredients instead). Alternatively, you could use the recipe as it is and eat the rest the following day. They all keep well, with the exception of Treasure in the Tide and Vegetable Tempura, both of which use batter. In these cases, make up the batter and only use half of it on the day required, keeping the rest in a jug in the fridge. The rest of the veggies could be set aside in the fridge too.

For the other recipes, you can either reheat them slowly on the hob or in a preheated moderate oven, covered with foil, for 20 minutes. If you're a one-person household, you could simply halve again, or keep the recipe for two people and take the remainder for lunch the following day. If there are no reheating facilities where you study/ work, I can highly recommend treating yourself to a food flask. I bought one at Sainsbury's for £9 and it has been used a lot. I know there is an initial outlay, but if you're like a lot of us and buy food out which you can't afford, you'll quickly recoup the money. If there are three of you, you could try a combination of waste avoidance techniques. When we went from a four to a three-person household in my family, for instance, we would take it in turns who ate the fourth portion for lunch the next day in said food flask, for instance, or sometimes we would have dinner comprised of two sets of leftovers and a salad. I am not a big fan of freezing meals if I can help it (please see below), but I did find the freezer useful for the wraps, crumpets or pittas left in the packet, or the half a loaf of bread. The important thing is to remember if you are tweaking a cookbook with recipes for four is to have a quick daily check of your fridge and cupboards, so you're not wasting food or money by accumulating surplus. I know this seems obvious, but it is a good habit to develop.

How to Get Your Best Value from This Book

If you need to maximise your savings, following the three week plan would be your best bet. However, if you find this too limiting, the book is replete with the application of frugal principles which you will be able to use without thinking about it; the work has already been done. This is because the thrifty habits of eating with the seasons, meal planning, food preparation, getting the maximum from ingredients, shopping around and creating a store cupboard (which is actually USED) run consistently throughout his book. How does this work in detail?

Eating with the Seasons

This book is divided into seasons so you can get your vegetables at their cheapest and tastiest. If you are lucky enough to be able to access a Farmers' Market, or a fruit and vegetables stall at your local market — although I haven't assumed that this is the case — you may well find it worth your while to do some price comparisons. I have found the seasonal vegetables at my Farmers' Market to be cheaper than that at the supermarket, but I don't shop exclusively there because I do like fruit such as oranges and pineapples which obviously don't grow in the UK. Because I don't know your individual circumstances, then, I have concentrated on supermarket shopping.

Meal Planning

Knowing what you are going to cook, then compiling a corresponding shopping list and sticking to it famously prevent unnecessary or unworkable purchases, but this takes energy we sometimes don't have, so I have done it for you! In EVERY week I include two-out-of-one dishes, either by doubling up a dish to be eaten over two days with varying accompaniments (such as a batch of ratatouille which is served in a pie on one day and with couscous on another), or by creating a base mixture which can be assembled and eaten in different ways. For example, the same hoisin-flavoured mince mixture is used in a hotpot one day and shaped into Hoisin Burgers the next. So even if you don't follow the whole plan, you can still benefit from multiple examples of double duty dishes.

Food Preparation

I don't know about you, but I used to be very good about cooking a large quantity of chickpeas (for example), popping them in portions in the freezer, then wondering what to do with them. Or I would cook enough rice for the meal we were eating and beyond, then subsequently forget about it. In this book, all those chickpeas, rice or whatever are apportioned within the week's recipes, so you need not worry about inspiration descending if you've had a challenging week.

Getting the Maximum from Ingredients

Boy, have I put my back into this one! Examples include:

- A tin of coconut milk yields water and cream, which separate in cold temperatures such as the inside of the fridge or on a winter's day; in this book, the coconut water binds the base of a sweet pie and the cream goes into its topping.

- A tin of chickpeas also has water (known as aquafaba), used by vegans in place of egg whites; I whip this up to make a meringue and process the chickpeas with other ingredients to make a hummus in the same High Tea.

- Half a bottle of cider is poured into a soup, the other into a savoury crumble.

- Half a packet of ready-made marinated tofu is an ingredient in the savoury muffin one day, the other half is part of a wrap filling the next.

- Pastry is rolled thinly to get two dinners from it: some tomato tarts and an asparagus flan.

- A 500g bag of sultanas is revisited for Rock Cakes, porridge recipes, ground rice and a loaf cake.

- A jar of peanut butter is stirred into a sauce, spread onto toast, bound with sweetcorn in a wrap...

- A knob of ginger is peeled and grated for sushi, a dipping sauce and a stew. No manky bits left in the fridge!

- A pot of yoghurt is opened for a sauce at dinner, then its remainder is used to stuff pears for breakfast the following morning.

- Six shells of six oranges are filled with trifles as a dessert; their flesh is blended with yoghurt and peaches to make an unusual Lassi; in turn, the rest of the yoghurt pot is the main component of a Raita in the same meal.

I could go on...

Shopping Around

When you look at the shopping lists, you will see that each list has two distinctive parts, font wise: the italicised ingredients can be found (hopefully) at your local supermarket (ASDA in my case). The rest were purchased at my local budget supermarket, Aldi. I hesitated about suggesting two shops; after all, this book is supposed to save you time as well as money. However, I found it was the only way I could stay on the right side of the agreed figure; when I asked as many people as I could – (including really busy ones who either worked long hours, had a large family or both) – if they would be willing to go to two shops if it saved them money, they all (without exception) said that they would, and did. They couldn't afford not to. But, of course, this is your call.

About the Prices

This book shows that you can eat well on a given budget while excluding all animal products, specifically while demonstrating, via shopping lists and menus, how this can be carried out. However, since the writing of the book, and a subsequent delay between the writing and the publication, prices have changed substantially. I mention price variation earlier in the Introduction, but as we are now facing a cost of living crisis, this variation has been wider than anticipated. I considered updating all the prices, but decided it would be counter-productive for the following reasons:

- Hopefully (!) the cost of living crisis we are in at the time of writing (May 2024) will end at some point;

- Prices and the availability of products change constantly;

- If you follow the shopping lists and menus, your spending will still stay within a money-saving parameter, because ingredients aren't being wasted;

- Choices for vegans have hugely improved over the last five years. One of the consequences this has meant you can now get vegan goods from budget supermarkets which were previously unavailable, at least in the UK (see below);

- As demand for plant-based foods has increased, some prices have, even in these times, decreased. For instance, you can currently buy Sainsbury's own vegan mayo (Plant Pioneers) for £1.30. I costed vegan mayo at £2 when writing this book, because own brand vegan mayos were rare at the time and that was the lowest price I could find;

- The development of vegan cuisine has increased at a rapid pace; for instance, there is no longer a need to buy expensive egg replacers - (see below) - and experiments are ongoing in the sphere of plant-based cooking.

Moreover, with some adjustments, you may (I say "may" because prices are still fluctuating widely) be able to keep the total around the one specified in the shopping lists. Here are some thoughts….

Make Use of the Foods Now Available at Budget Supermarkets

You can now find vegan cheese, yoghurt, sausages, burgers, flax seeds (more on these below), plant milks, vegan brioche buns and nan breads without dairy at Aldi and/or Lidl. For example, you can still find several varieties of vegan sausages for around £2 or under in Aldi. It's also worth noting that you can still find a 45p wholemeal loaf there for when you're stretched financially (and at Sainsbury's and Tesco too). Therefore, by buying the majority of your groceries at the budget supermarket, you should still be within (or not far from) the total originally given.

On Fruit and Veg at Budget Supermarkets

The availability of ingredients can be a postcode lottery, but, generally speaking, more kinds of veg are appearing at the discount supermarkets than could be found a few years ago. To give just one example, in the shopping list alluded to below, £1.10 is quoted for a pack of baby spinach in a main supermarket; yesterday I found a 240g pack for 99p at Aldi. Additionally, of course, there are always the bargains to be had at the front of the fruit and veg section in both budget supermarkets. (I was particularly pleased this week with three bulbs of garlic for 49p). In addition to these bargains, there are often special deals (check out www.hotukdeals.com as well as, obviously, the shops' flyers).

Organic or Non-Organic?

In my shopping lists I have organic onions and potatoes. I have no longer been able to find these in my local Aldi. (Your experience may be similar). The plus side is that the non-organic options are much cheaper; their onions are only 65p for 1kg, their "Wonky" potatoes are just 80p for 2.5kg.

In an ideal world, I would always buy organic, but we don't live in an ideal world, especially if we're constrained by our budgets. So it is worth familiarising yourself with the "Dirty Dozen" if you haven't already; these are the plant foods that it is best to buy organically if at all possible. Potatoes and onions don't appear on the Dirty Dozen List as I write, so if savings need to be made, it would be better to make them on these veggies. For an up-to-date list of the twelve plants on the list, check out Pesticide Action UK.

Finding Alternatives

Lemons
In my shopping lists, I have single lemons, giving the price as 29p. However, budget supermarkets now sell lemons in a net of four, at least where I live, for around 65p. Fortunately, I use lemons frequently, so they will appear in the subsequent weeks (see "Autumn Recipes, Week One"). If you keep the lemons in a plastic bag in the fridge, they will last for a month. And the good news is they work out at around 16p each.

Egg Replacers
Commercial egg replacers are good, but expensive. You can make a cheaper egg replacer by mixing 1 tbs flax seeds with 3 tbs of hot water, letting it stand for ten minutes, then using this gelatinous substance in your recipe. This is the equivalent of one egg. If you are making batter, up the ratio of plant milk and baking powder to the flour. So in my "Treasure in the Tide" recipe, use 2 tsp baking powder instead of 1 tsp, and 480ml of plant milk, not the 350 ml given, if you wish to skip the pricier egg replacer.

Shopping Around
I address this earlier, concluding that some people simply can't afford to only use one supermarket. How much you shop around is, of course, your call, but if an alternative shop isn't far away, it can save you a lot of money. I noticed the price of tahini has increased dramatically in most places, but found it at the price I quoted (£1.80) in Morrisons. Sometimes we don't have the money to save time.

Swapping Out Bread Products

Toppings can be put on anything, from bagels to crumpets. If what I have specified will not allow you to keep within budget, you can obviously put your own spin on the recipe. Crumpets are currently cheaper than bread muffins, for example. And it goes without saying the bread products are regularly reduced, especially at the end of the day, when they are often marked down to pennies.

Putting the Strategies to the Test

I applied the above strategies to a shopping list from my "Autumn Recipes" chapter. I was able to stay within the total I originally provided, actually saving the grand total of 26p!

It is my sincerest wish that, even in these times, you find a thrifty friend in what follows...

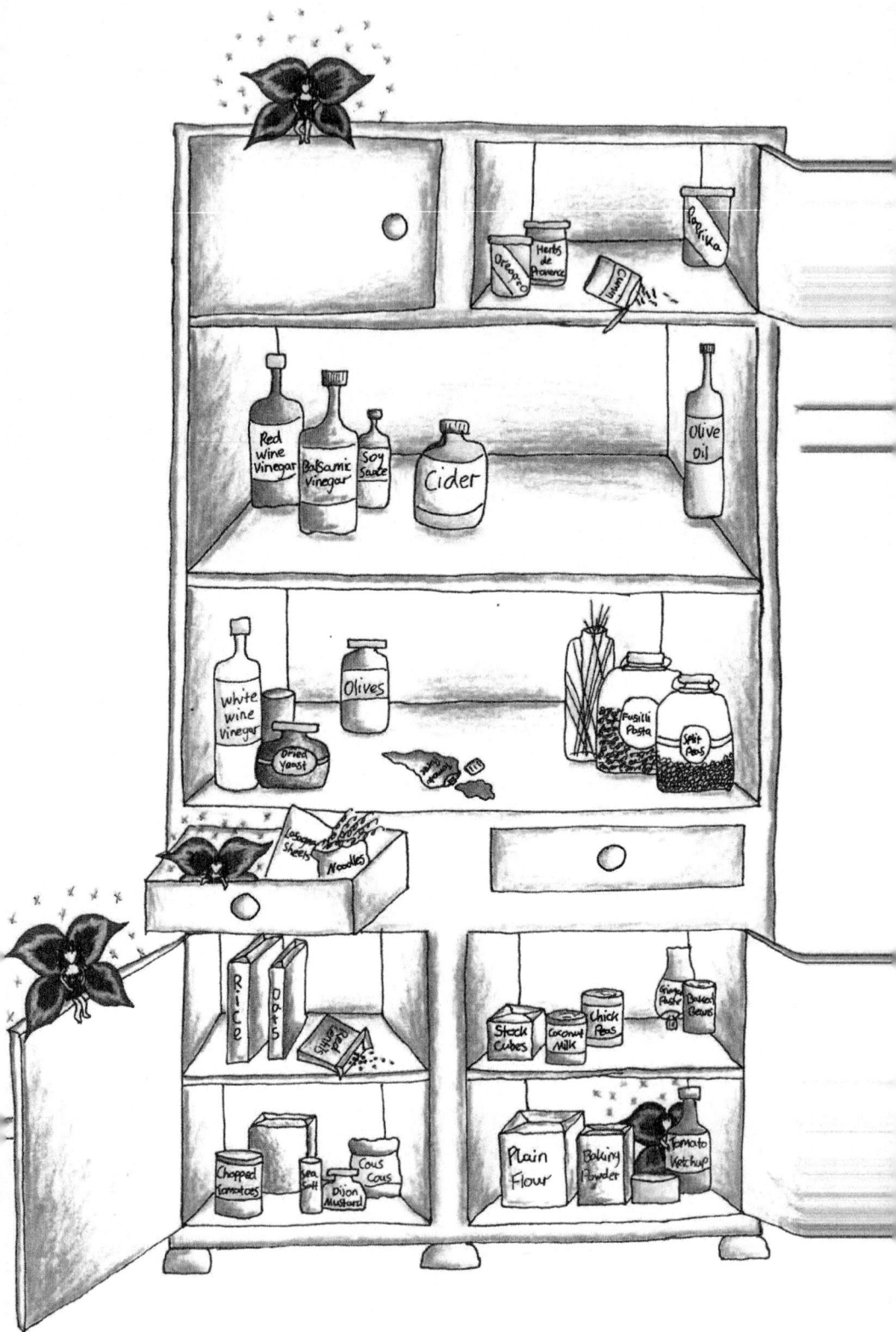

The Store Cupboard (In an Ideal World...)

By store cupboard, I mean anywhere you store food, be it fridge, freezer, cupboard or, in my case, the space under the stairs, because I always had a fantasy about a walk-in food cupboard, which couldn't happen in my terraced house, so I relocated most of the equipment already there and created a larder. I can just about stand up in it.

How do you build up a store cupboard which really works for you and actually gets used? I have wondered this many times, and wasted a lot of money in the process. Now, the number one question I ask myself is: what are my cooking patterns (or the cooking patterns I wish to adopt)? I still can't remember why I bought the tin of chestnut puree sitting forlornly in my cupboard – all I know is I must find a use for it within the next two years. I have since told myself that I will not buy anything again unless I know what I am going to use it for – which means writing down the title of the recipe which attracted me (and where I found it) on my calendar. I also challenged myself to compile a list which, from experience, I know will get eaten or used in recipes, both regularly and irregularly. Maybe yours will look like this list below, or be completely different, but I have yet to meet anyone who never uses tinned tomatoes.

Store Cupboard in an Ideal World – Regularly Used Ingredients:

Apple sauce; baked beans; baking powder; balsamic vinegar; bicarbonate of soda; coconut milk; cornflour; curry paste; custard (vegan); dried mushrooms; flour; jam; lemon juice; lentils; long life plant milks; marmalade; Marmite; mayonnaise (vegan); mirin; mustard; mustard powder; noodles (dried); oats; olives in brine; olive oil; pasta; quinoa; peanut butter; passata; pasta; pearl barley; pesto (vegan); red wine vinegar; rice; rice vinegar; soy sauce; split peas; sugar; sultanas; vanilla essence; tamari; teriyaki sauce; Thai curry pastes; tins of tomatoes; tins of chickpeas (or dried ones); tomato ketchup; tomato puree;

vacuum packed gnocchi; various beans, dried or tinned: black beans, black-eyed beans, butter beans, cannellini beans, mixed beans and kidney beans; white wine vinegar; Worcestershire sauce (vegan).

Store Cupboard in an Ideal World – Irregularly Used Ingredients:

Buckwheat flour; chipotle paste; dried onions; dried garlic; gram flour; harissa paste; hoisin sauce; nori sheets; pickles; sushi rice; sundried tomato paste; tinned fruit.

Stocking the Store Cupboard (AKA the Wherewithal Cupboard)

When money is tight, this obviously has to be a gradual thing; that is why the shopping lists in this book build up your stock week by week, and within the week's budget. However, when funds allow, it is worth stocking up on staples – such as those listed above – but yours may be different – so that you always have the wherewithal to produce a meal. In fact, I now think of my cupboard as a Wherewithal Cupboard: the basics of a dinner, plus fresh vegetables/fruit.

For example, if I always have tins of tomatoes, tomato puree, coconut milk and curry paste in my stores, I know I'll have the means to produce a basic curry, once I've bought the veg. When irregularly used ingredients are used for a specific recipe, I make sure I research more ways of using it so it doesn't go off before I can get to it (although that tin of chestnut puree is still waiting to be rescued). That is why you won't see an ingredient making a one-off appearance in this book.

A Word about Herbs and Spices

If I could only take one pot of herbs and one jar of spice to a deserted island (where vegans spend a lot of time, apparently) it would be, without doubt, mixed dried herbs and cumin, respectively. The former because it would cover most bases and the latter because cumin appears in so many cuisines: Middle Eastern, North African, Indian, Central American and South American and, naturally, therefore, in many fusion recipes. Again, when shopping, the Golden Rule of Store Cupboards applies in thrifty living: before buying a new herb/spice, have more than one idea about what you're going to do with it. I know it's easier said than done, but it is rewarding to have much-used jars as opposed to dusty ones in your cupboard. Again, I try to give you a helping hand in this book by ensuring that no jar only gets to leave the cupboard only once.

Stocking the Fridge and Freezer

I am really talking to myself here, but I think it is especially important to be strict with yourself about knowing the future purpose of ingredients for the fridge in the short term because they are, obviously, perishable. The exception would be miso, which lasts almost indefinitely, and opened condiments and pickles. Know which vegetables you are going to use in which dishes before you purchase them. I speak from experience, as I have an especial weakness for vegetables. I just think they're beautiful. Of course, if you have succumbed to some gorgeous specimens without having a plan for them, you could always do a 'clean up the fridge' type meal like a vegetable curry, stew, soup, mixed veggie rice, casserole or stir-fry. All except the latter keep well too, and taste even better the next day. Apart from vegetables, I always tend to have margarine, small packets of nuts (it isn't worth buying large bags of nuts unless you have a specific idea for them in mind; nuts go rancid quickly) and plant milk, with regular appearances of vegan cheese, vegan crème fraiche and tofu (but only if I know what I am going to do with them). Naturally, all the fridge items in the shopping lists in this book have designated uses, with no half or quarter packets hanging around, destined to go off.

You can be more flexible about planning with the freezer – when the money is there of course – as you have more time to play with. The freezer is so useful for storing batches of cooked pulses (please see, for example, under 'Food Preparation'); for packets of frozen fruit for overnight oats; for veggies such as peas, edamame beans, okra and sweetcorn, and for bread bargains. I think we all know this one; at the end of the super-market's working day, especially on Monday nights — in my local shop anyway — loaves, rolls, pitta breads, baguettes etc. can go for as little as 10p. And don't ignore posher shops like Marks and Spencer; in my home town, there are great bargains to be had on a Thursday night with the usually more expensive loaves of pave, focaccia and ciabatta.

You may disagree with me on this, but I am not a fan of freezing whole meals; I often don't like what it does to the texture and flavour of the veggies, especially potatoes. But needs must, I know, and sometimes it is unavoidable, if you know you're not going to get to the leftovers in the fridge before they go off. But personally I keep this strategy as a last resort.

Regarding processed foods for the freezer, I think we all know they should be kept to a minimum, but the presence of veggie sausages, gyoza (Japanese vegetable dumplings), veggie or fishless fingers and meat-free mince can be a such a relief if you're short on time, and you can stock up if you happen to have enough spare cash when there are bargains to be had.

The Magical Store Cupboard

Doesn't exist. Everything has to be bought, apart from food gifts. That's why I insisted on factoring in the cost of store cupboard items as well as fresh food. But there is something a bit magical about being able to conjure up a meal from your supplies, so it goes without saying that, whenever financially feasible, it pays to buy your staples in bulk (either economy sizes whose contents are cheaper per 100g or items on offer which will keep or can be frozen). If you want to ask someone to eat impromptu, or if your children forget to tell you they invited a friend over ("I said you wouldn't mind..."), it is good to know you have your Wherewithal Cupboard and freezer. Maybe you could knock up some Haricot Crepes (all from store cupboard ingredients), Spaghetti Bolognaise (you can rehydrate dried mushrooms if you like mushrooms in your Spag Bol and have none fresh) or an Okra and Pea Curry (using curry paste, tomatoes and coconut milk from your cupboard, and the vegetables from your freezer). I am not breaking my own rule and assuming you will always have these items in; what I am saying, however, is that when you do have a little flexibility with your funds, it is liberating to be able to 'expect the unexpected' and stock up because you enjoy having the freedom for some planned spontaneity. For this reason, I like to have jars of dried onion and garlic in for the times when I'm out of fresh. Invaluable!

Ten More Ways to Maximise Your Food on a Minimal Budget

1. Did you know carrots last longer if you cut the tops off? (Now that is magical...)

2. Sprouting seeds takes pennies but gives maximised nutrients because the seed uses them to sprout and grow. Punch a few holes in the top of a washed jar (I tend to use the large olive ones), pop your seeds (broccoli, radish, etc.) in the bottom, swill with water and drain through the holes. Repeat once a day for about 3 days and watch them sprout!

3. Buying in bulk is not always feasible if you don't have the money upfront, but it can work if you have a friend or neighbour to divide the cost with. Great for 'Buy One, Get One Free' too; I message my friend when I'm shopping to see if she's interested in any finds I come across.

4. Basil and parsley (on the windowsill or a garden if you have one) are especially useful because they can be grown (from those pots you get in the supermarket, then transplanted) from spring through to the autumn and spread quickly. Parsley is great to put in salads and sauces, and basil is delicious in your own pesto; I just make one by whizzing up a lot of leaves with whichever nuts are cheapest at the time and adding a little oil and seasonings.

5. Pearl barley, at 55p for 500g at the time of writing, is perhaps the thriftiest grain there is; not only is it a useful source of iron (amongst other nutrients), it also makes a comforting addition to soups, stews and salads because it is so satiating. So if you have leftover veggies that

need eating up quickly, it is very handy to have this in the cupboard.

6. One investment I highly recommend making is an immersion blender (sometimes called a stick blender), which you can still find for a tenner. It whizzes up soup from leftover veggies with stock or coconut milk and spices in seconds, with hardly any washing up. If you have some reduced priced bread in the freezer for some toast on the side, it can almost feel that you have magically created a meal from thin air!

7. Going to the market at the end of the day yields fabulous fruit bargains – about the only time I can get punnets of berries for a pound, or sometimes even two punnets.

8. Big packets of vegetable gyoza (stuffed Japanese pancakes), soy sauce, Japanese Yuzu dressing, jasmine rice, filo squares for spring rolls and hoisin sauce are, likewise, cheaper at my local Korean/Japanese/Thai/Chinese mini supermarket. Again, if you are lucky enough to have one, pop in when time allows and do a few price comparisons.

9. Pulses, basmati rice, poppadoms, spices, and coconut milk are invariably cheaper at my local grocer than they are at the supermarket. If there is one near you, check it out! The corner shop isn't always more expensive.

10. Imported vegetables like plantain and okra are often non-existent at my local supermarket, or are very expensive. Specialist grocers like the ones mentioned above not only stock them, but also, frequently, at enticingly affordable prices.

As I wanted this book to be useful to everyone, I could not presume you are lucky enough to have access to shops like those above, so I deliberately stuck to food found in supermarkets. But if you can shave more off our already frugal budget, fusion food will be even more magical.

Now, please let me introduce you to the alchemy of Frugal Fusion Food...

Winter Recipes

Dinners for Winter, Week One

1. Five Onion Teriyaki Soup and Herby Scones
2. Emoji Pie with a Hint of Moroccan Flavours
3. Superfast Broad Bean with Giant Tofu Croutons
4. Savoury Crumble with Pickled Onions and Cider Braised Vegetables
5. Goreng Meets Goulash
6. Mock Moussaka with Peas
7. Stovetop Mock Moussaka with Pepper and Broad Bean Salad

Cooking Chickpeas

The Mock Moussaka requires cooked chickpeas, which are also used in this week's lunches; you'll save a lot of time (and cash) if you cook a 500g batch of dry chickpeas. Soak them the night before Day One, then on Day One, bring them to boil in a large pan of water and boil vigorously for ten minutes. Turn down the heat, and boil just above a simmer for an hour. When you can squash a (COOLED!) chickpea on the roof of your mouth, you can assume the rest are done. As an alternative to the cold soak, bring a pan of chickpeas to boil, boil hard for five minutes, then soak in hot water for an hour. Drain, add more water to cover copiously, then boil for at least an hour as above. Drain and cool. You should now have approximately 1 kg to 1.1 kg cooked chickpeas. You can, should you wish, apportion the chickpeas so that you're ready for future dinners and lunches. If the portion is going in the fridge, use a sealed container or a bowl with a plate on top. If it is going in the freezer, make sure you leave a margin at the top of your container for a little expansion (about 3cm).

1) Reserve 4 rounded tablespoons of cooked chickpeas for Day 2's dinner.

2) Freeze 6 rounded tablespoons of cooked chickpeas for the Moussaka which will be your dinner on Days 6 and 7.

3) Refrigerate 8 tablespoons chickpeas in readiness for Day 3's lunch.

4) Freeze 500g cooked chickpeas in preparation for Day 4's hummus at lunch time.

5) Freeze 8 heaped chickpeas for Day 7's lunch.

6) Freeze anything left over – chickpeas always come in handy!

Shopping List for Dinners for Winter, Week One

	Prices (£)
Vegetables/Fruit	
30g chives	00.49
1 large aubergine	00.68
750g mushrooms	01.59
1 packet of 3 mixed peppers	00.92
750g organic onions	00.95
500g organic potatoes	01.39
fresh parsley	00.69
spring onions	00.47
600g parsnips	00.45
759g organic carrots	00.95
130g baby corn	00.99
400g shallots	00.71
mixed chillies	00.57
1.5kg organic potatoes	01.39
650g mushrooms (e.g. Aldi)	01.40
1 garlic bulb	00.30
225g green beans	00.95
One large leek	00.44
Fridge	
1 litre plant milk	00.59
2 x 200g extra mature vegan cheddar @ £2 each	04.00
vegan margarine	00.85
500g vegan coconut yoghurt	01.50
396g firm tofu	01.50
Cupboard	
1.5kg plain flour	00.45
170g baking powder	00.69
568ml cider	00.85

4 tins chopped tomatoes	01.36
tomato puree	00.37
1 kg porridge oats	00.75
150g mixed nuts	01.29
turmeric	00.49
paprika	00.49
soy sauce	00.42
Dijon mustard	00.47
275 long grain brown rice	00.99
500g soft brown sugar	00.69
200g peanuts	00.29
500g cornflour	00.85
150g sliced (flaked) almonds	01.39
cumin	00.49
13g dried mint	00.69
olive oil	01.20
500g dried chickpeas	00.75
teriyaki sauce	00.95
nutmeg	00.70
80g tube sundried tomato puree	00.75
227g jar cocktail onions	00.90
57g mustard powder	01.34
dried mixed herbs	00.30
Freezer	
907g 1 packet frozen peas	00.55
750g 1 packet frozen broad beans	01.35
175g packet of plant Shawarma	02.50
TOTAL	**£47.41**

Five Onion Teriyaki Soup and Herby Scones

There are so many delicious onion soup recipes, but a lot of them rely on a rather expensive combination of two or more types of alcohol and a pricey beef stock. If you are watching the pennies, cider will tenderise and sweeten the onions just as well. Apart from providing its own flavour, the teriyaki sauce unites all the ingredients: it tempers the taste of the alcohol, releases the tang in the onions and colours the whole a rich brown. As with all recipes which include flour and alcohol, it is essential to provide enough cooking time so that the alcohol is reduced and the flour thickens the soup without leaving a floury aftertaste. This is a superlative onion soup. Start the scones first if this is more convenient for you; alternatively, see below.

Ingredients for the Soup

1 large leek, washed and chopped

150g organic shallots, peeled and chopped

2 large white onions, peeled and chopped

4 cloves garlic, peeled and chopped finely

Half a bunch of spring onions, tops removed, then chopped into short lengths (including the green)

1 tablespoon flour

1 tablespoon teriyaki sauce

500ml water

250 ml organic cider (half a 500ml bottle – remainder used this week in the Savoury Crumble with Pickled Onions and Cider Braised Vegetables)

3 tablespoons olive oil

Method

1) Put the oil in a large wok and add the leek, shallots, white onion and spring onions. Fry for about 4 minutes until slightly under tender.

2) Add the flour and mix thoroughly to coat all the ingredients. Fry for 5 minutes, stirring frequently.

3) Add the garlic and 1 tablespoon teriyaki sauce, then fry for another 5 minutes on a low heat.

4) Slowly pour in the water, the other 1 tablespoon teriyaki sauce and cider, stirring furiously.

5) Bring to the boil, turn the heat down, then simmer for 15–20 minutes until the taste of the alcohol is 'cooked off' – you will need to taste it.

6) Prepare the scones while the soup is simmering; turn off the heat while you are finishing the baking and reheat when you are about to take the scones out of the oven.

Herby Scones with Parsley Spread

Ingredients

For the Scones
225g plain flour
4 teaspoons baking powder
50g vegan margarine from the fridge
2 teaspoons dried herbs
1 teaspoon mustard powder
8–10 tablespoon plant milk

A little extra milk to glaze if you use all of the above

For the Parsley Spread
50g vegan margarine
Tiny pinch of mustard powder
1 packet 30g parsley, washed and chopped.

Method

1) Preheat the oven to 230°C/450°F/Gas Mark 8 if you haven't done so already. Grease a baking sheet.

2) Sift the flour, mustard powder and baking powder into a bowl. Break up the margarine with a spoon into little dots then rub in the flour with your fingertips. It does make a difference if the margarine is very cold, because when the scones are baked, the steam created will inject some air and make them light.

3) Stir in the herbs, then gradually add the plant milk until you have a soft but not sloppy dough.

4) Flour a board, shape the dough into a ball, then roll it out to a thickness of about 2 cm.

5) Cut out your favourite shape according to which cutters you have – I like little flowers – then gather all the trimmings, roll out and cut again until you have used all the dough (or as much as possible – any bits can be just roughly shaped with your hands).

6) Put the scones on the greased baking sheet and glaze with plant milk.

7) Bake for 12–15 minutes until golden brown.

8) While they are cooling slightly, beat the parsley and mustard powder into the margarine with a fork then put into a little bowl.

9) Put the onion soup into individual bowls and serve the scones separately.

If you're feeling too tired to make the scones, you could just serve this with toast. Or you could make the scone dough the night before, and just proceed from Step 4. Or, if you think you'll want to make this again in the future, you could even freeze the dough up to two months in advance. Let it defrost in the fridge the night before.

Emoji Pie with a Hint of Moroccan Flavours

This would be a lovely pie to make for a friend who is going through a rough time. If the gorgeous blend of almonds, chickpeas, paprika, mint and cumin, Moroccan style, doesn't elicit a smile, maybe the happy face will!

Ingredients

500g tin of chopped tomatoes

4 rounded tablespoons of cooked chickpeas

1 teaspoon cumin

2 teaspoon dried mint

1 teaspoon paprika

100g sliced almonds

2 tablespoons tomato puree

1 chilli, chopped

700g potatoes

20g margarine

1 tablespoon plant milk

1 tablespoon flour

Method

1) Peel the potatoes and cut into uniform pieces, then boil for approximately 20 minutes. Preheat the oven to Gas Mark 6/200°C/400°F.

2) While these are cooking, tip the tin of tomatoes and their juice into a bowl and roughly mash them with a fork. Pour into a non-stick pan.

3) Add the chickpeas, cumin, paprika, mint, tomato puree, almonds and chilli. Stir well, then simmer for 10 minutes.

4) Transfer the chickpea mixture into an ovenproof dish. Mash the cooked potatoes with the margarine and milk, then reserve a couple of tablespoons. Spread some flour over a large chopping board, put the reserved potatoes in the middle, then gently roll into a ball so it becomes coated with flour. If you like, mould facial features according to your fancy between the flats of your hands. If you want to make hair, push the potato through a garlic crusher.

5) Spread the rest of the potato on top of the chickpea mixture. Add the face, then lightly brown in the oven for about 15–20 minutes.

6) Serve with a smile of your own!

Superfast Broad Bean with Giant Tofu Croutons

When you feel that winter is losing its novelty value, and you want a preview of spring, this will give you a taste of what is to come with a frozen/tinned version of spring vegetables. They are none the less flavoursome for that, especially when well-seasoned, and will give you dinner in under 15 minutes. You can buy tofu already fried, and if I happen to be in an area which has Chinese/Thai shop this is what I will buy, but you can use supermarket tofu provided you drain it well before frying.

Ingredients

Giant Tofu Croutons
349g packet firm tofu
4 tablespoons flour
1 teaspoon salt
1 teaspoon freshly ground black pepper
Enough oil to create a 1cm pool at the bottom of your chosen pan

Superfast Broad Bean
4 tablespoons frozen peas
4 tablespoons frozen broad beans (do not thaw)
2 tablespoons tomato puree
1 tin chopped tomatoes
2 tablespoons sundried tomato puree
Cloves garlic, finely chopped
2 medium onions, chopped
1 packet baby corn
150g mushrooms

Method

1) Put the tofu on a large plate. Put another plate on top, then a weight such as a heavy book. Leave until Step 5; this will squeeze excess water out.

2) Fry the onion until transparent. Add the rest of the ingredients, and stir thoroughly.

3) Bring to the boil, and simmer for about 10 minutes until the vegetables are tender, with the exception of the baby corn, which is better al dente in this dish. If you have kept the peas and broad beans frozen, they shouldn't overcook by the time the mushrooms and baby corn are ready.

4) Keep on a very low light, stirring occasionally, while you make the croutons:

5) Lift off the weight and plate, drain away the water, then cut the tofu into 5cm squares. Place flour in a shallow dish and season with salt and pepper. Dust the tofu with flour one piece at a time, pressing it into the flour on both sides. Heat 1cm oil in a large frying pan over medium heat. Cook tofu, in 2 batches, for 1 minute each side or until crisp and golden, then drain on paper towel.

6) Serve the stew surrounded by the croutons.

NB: Often avowed tofu haters like these crispy croutons.

Savoury Crumble with Pickled Onions and Cider Braised Veg

This took a lot of experimentation before reaching the desired effects: cider-infused tender vegetables with a tangy pickle, topped by an intensely savoury, crunchy topping. Really the only way of achieving this is to divide the layers into two parts: braising the veg overnight (or all day if you are at home), then putting on the topping immediately before you are due to speedily bake it on a high temperature. Otherwise, the underside of the topping is unpleasantly soggy. Conversely, now is not the time for the vegetables to be al dente, so they need a very, very long and slow braising. It is honestly worth it; each mouthful is a surprise.

Ingredients

Topping
55g porridge oats
55g chopped mixed nuts
100g vegan cheddar
30g vegan margarine
55g plain flour

Braised Veg
2 medium parsnips, cut into large chunks,
2 medium carrots, cut into large slices

4 tbs frozen peas
500g mushrooms, washed and quartered
6 medium pickled onions
250ml water
1 tbs cornflour
1 tsp mustard
2 tbs teriyaki sauce
250 ml cider (the other half of the bottle bought for this week's soup)

Method

1) Before you go to bed, or early in the morning, put the oven on its lowest possible setting. Put the veg and pickled onions into a shallow casserole dish, and toss them until they are well combined.

2) Pour the cornflour into a pan, whisk the mustard and teriyaki sauce into the water, then gradually add this and the cider until you have a smooth sauce. Continue to add slowly until it is all incorporated, then bring to the boil. Simmer for five minutes, then pour over the vegetables.

3) Put everything into the oven overnight; if your casserole dish doesn't have a lid, cover it with foil. It will happily cook for eight hours. Put it aside until you are ready to use it; if this is going to several hours away, put it in the fridge.

4) When you are ready to make the dish, take the veg out of the fridge (if you used it) then put them into a shallow dish. Turn the oven on to Gas Mark 7/220/430C. Leave it for 15 minutes to heat up.

5) In the meantime, rub the marg into the flour until it resembles breadcrumbs. Add the chopped mixed nuts, oats and vegan cheddar and sprinkle over the veg.

6) Cook for 15 minutes in your hot oven until browned.

Goreng Meets Goulash

Nasi Goreng and Goulash have at least paprika and beef in common, so I came to the unlikely conclusion that you could combine the two, vegan style. Unlikely it may be, but it was utterly delicious.

Ingredients

For the paste
2 garlic cloves, peeled
a pinch of nutmeg
Pinch ground turmeric
¼ teaspoon freshly ground black pepper
3 shallots, peeled and chopped
30g salted peanuts
2 red chillies, seeds removed
1 tablespoon soft brown sugar
1–2 tablespoons olive oil

For the stir-fry
1 teaspoon paprika
1 30g (ish) packet of chives; reserve a few blades for decoration
1 tablespoon oil
150g mushrooms, sliced

1 175g packet plant Shawarma-style strips
225g fine green beans, trimmed and sliced into 1cm/½in pieces
275g cooked, cooled long grain brown rice
1 tablespoon sweet soy sauce (otherwise known as *ketjap manis, an Indonesian soy sauce). *It is cheaper to make your own mix.
1 tablespoon dark soy sauce mixed with 1 tablespoon soft brown sugar. Bring to the boil, stirring all the time, then boil for 5 minutes.

Garnish
1 tablespoon vegan coconut yoghurt and snipped chives.

Method

1) Make the paste by whizzing all the ingredients together in a food processor until you have a fairly smooth consistency; don't worry if there are little bits of peanut, but everything else should be well blended. Put to one side.

2) Sprinkle the plant Shawarma-style strips with the paprika and then fry in the oil for five minutes, lifting and tossing the strips so that they don't catch.

3) Add the mushrooms, chives and beans and fry for a further five minutes, keeping the ingredients moving as before. Add the paste and stir-fry vigorously for two minutes to enable all the ingredients to thoroughly absorb it.

4) Add the rice and ketjap manis and stir-fry for two minutes so that everything is mixed and heated through.

5) Serve garnished with vegan coconut yoghurt and snipped chives.

Mock Moussaka

NB: This requires cooked chickpeas (please see the note on this week's list of dinners). If that hasn't been possible to arrange, you'll need two tins. On the second night, you can prepare the salad while the moussaka is reheating.

This will feed four people for two days (or unexpected guests). It has similar layers to a moussaka, but the resemblance stops there; a pungent vegan cheese sauce is used and a sweet, tangy tomato and chickpea layer replaces the mince. When I have served this to guests, without exception they have come back for seconds, even the most impassioned meat-eaters, such is its hearty depth of mixed delights. It is quite a performance to make, so it is best reserved for your day off. Alternatively, you can make it the evening before, omitting the baking stage, and leave the assembled dish in the fridge until you come home the following day, but take it out as soon as you get in the door so you can allow it to come to room temperature before baking. Turn the oven on 15 minutes before baking.

Ingredients

1 large, or two small aubergines
2 tablespoons olive oil (or thereabouts)
2 tins chopped tomatoes
1 cloves garlic, chopped
1 onion, chopped
6 tablespoons precooked chickpeas (or two drained tins)
200g mushrooms, thinly sliced
1 red pepper, chopped
1 yellow pepper, chopped
800g organic potatoes
4 tablespoons tomato puree
1 teaspoon dried mixed herbs
salt to taste

170g vegan cheddar cheese (one block of 55g, grated with the smallest hole on the grater, and 115g for the cheese sauce)
1 tablespoon plain flour
30g vegan margarine
1 heaped teaspoon Dijon mustard
1 teaspoon dried mustard
500ml plant milk

Method

1) First prepare the aubergine(s): line two large plates with kitchen paper. Slice into 1cm slices, then fry in the oil until soft and lightly browned on both sides. Aubergines are notorious for soaking up oil;

two tricks help with this. Firstly, if you are lucky enough to have a griddle pan, you can brush the pan with oil and if you keep an eye out, turning the aubergine frequently, you should be able to soften the aubergine without needing to add more oil. Secondly, if you fry the aubergine in two batches, once with the larger slices then again with the smaller (when you need less oil), hopefully they will cook evenly and you won't be forced to add more oil to prevent the little slices blackening.

2) Drain the cooked aubergine on the lined plates. When they are cool, blot them further with kitchen paper – this ensures that you extract as much oil as possible. Set aside.

3) Preheat the oven to 180°C/350°F/Gas Mark 4. Boil or steam the potatoes for about 15 minutes, until tender. Thick slices work well in this dish, so you need to cook them first.

4) While the potatoes are cooking, make the savoury tomato sauce: fry the onion until transparent, then add the peppers, garlic, tomatoes, tomato puree, herbs and chickpeas and salt (if necessary). Bring to boil, simmer for 10 minutes, then add the mushrooms and simmer for a further 5 minutes.

5) Pour the sauce into a large casserole dish. Lightly sprinkle with a little of the 55g block of vegan cheese. Add a layer of cooked potatoes (it doesn't matter if they overlap as they are already cooked), then sprinkle with a soft dusting of the vegan cheese. Finish with a layer of aubergines and another smidgeon of vegan cheese.

6) Repeat these layers, ending with the aubergine, but on this final layer do not sprinkle any cheese because you will be finishing with a covering of cheese sauce.

7) To make the cheese sauce, melt the margarine, add the flour and stir vigorously to make a smooth paste.

8) Turn off the heat, then very gradually, drop by drop, add the plant milk, stirring and scraping the sides and bottom of the pan after each addition. Turn on the heat and stir constantly until you have a thickened, smooth sauce. Add the Dijon mustard, dried mustard and the grated 115g portion of cheese and stir until both are incorporated.

9) Pour the sauce on the top of your layered casserole dish and bake for about 40 minutes until the top is lightly browned.

10) Serve with cooked peas (take 6 tablespoons from the freezer) on one night and a Pepper and Broad Bean salad the next. Thaw 4 tablespoons frozen broad beans, then combine with a chopped pepper (the remaining one from the pack) and four grated carrots. Sprinkle with a little soy sauce.

Suggestions for Breakfasts and Lunches for Winter, Week One

BREAKFASTS

Apple and Sultana Porridge

Mango and Apple Overnight Oats

Teriyaki Mushrooms on Toast

Parsnip Hash Browns with Garlic Tomatoes

Teriyaki Beans on Muffins with Indian Spiced Tofu and Tomatoes

Persian Rock Cakes — first half of batch

Persian Rock Cakes — second half of batch

LUNCHES

Muffins Stuffed with Indian Spiced Tofu and Tomato

Corn, Carrot and Peanut Tacos

Minted Mashed Chickpea and Beetroot Taquitos

Rolls with Hummus, Lettuce and Grated Carrot

Peanut Butter and Spiced Apple Sandwiches

Pixie Ploughman's with Chorizo

Smashed Teriyaki Chickpeas and Chopped Apple Sandwiches

Shopping List

	Prices (£)
8 apples	00.79
300g closed cup mushrooms	00.79
135g baby corn	00.89
270g apple sauce	00.45
6 crumpets	00.35
4 toasting muffins	00.39
4 large brown rolls	00.49
800g wholemeal bread	01.00
2 x 410g baked beans	00.46
500g sultanas	00.88
Peanuts	00.29
One lemon	00.29
	01.00
8 tortilla wraps	00.89
Round lettuce	00.40
2 x 250g cherry tomatoes	01.06
One mango	00.49
340g baby beetroot in vinegar	00.65
120g mini breadsticks	01.30
300g vegan chorizo sausages	02.00
340g peanut butter	00.65
349 tofu	01.59
TOTAL	**£16.73**
DINNERS	**£47.41**
TOTAL WITH DINNERS	**£64.14**

Already accounted for: plain flour, baking powder, brown sugar, teriyaki sauce, cooked chickpeas, mint and parsnips.

Notes on Breakfasts and Lunches for Winter, Week One

NB: From Day 3, lunches require cooked chickpeas. Please see the note on this week's list of dinners. If you're following the plan, you will already have the chickpeas in the refrigerator for Day 3. If not, you need to allow for this by cooking some on Day 2 or buying a tin. At the end of Day 3, remove the 500g of cooked chickpeas for Day 4's hummus; otherwise, again, you will need to allow for this, or buy some ready-made hummus.

   At the end of Day 6, remove the 8 heaped tablespoons cooked chickpeas from the freezer for Day 7's lunch.

Apple and Sultana Porridge
Stir half a chopped apple and 1 heaped tablespoon of sultanas into each porridge bowl.

Mango and Apple Overnight Oats
Stir 4 teaspoon applesauce and the flesh of a mango into your overnight oats before dividing into bowls.

Teriyaki Mushrooms on Toast
Lightly fry some mushrooms in 2 teaspoon oil until cooked but still quite firm, then stir-fry for another 2 minutes with 2 tablespoons teriyaki sauce, and pile onto toast.

Parsnip Hash Browns with Garlic Tomatoes
Grate 4 parsnips (there will be some from the bag used for the savoury crumble this week) and squeeze out excess water in a tightly rolled tea towel. Chop two onions. Fry the onions in 2 tablespoons olive oil until translucent, then add the parsnips and continue to fry until they crisp up. In another pan, very lightly fry 2 chopped garlic cloves in a non-stick pan, then add 8 halved cherry tomatoes, mix thoroughly, and barely fry for just one minute. Top the hash browns with the tomatoes.

Teriyaki Beans on Muffins
Splash some teriyaki sauce onto your warmed beans on toasted muffins.

Persian Rock Cakes
This will make enough for two breakfasts, but as rock cakes aren't the best keepers, refresh the second batch in a warm (150°C/300°F/ Gas Mark 2) oven for 10 minutes covered in foil. Recipe follows.

Bread Muffins Stuffed with Indian Spiced Tofu and Tomato (start the night before)

Drain the tofu, put it on a plate, then top it with another plate and add a weight (e.g. tin of beans) on top. Leave for about an hour. Cut the tofu in slices, rub a non-stick pan with two garlic cloves, then batch fry the tofu in 2 tablespoons oil with 1 teaspoon each of turmeric and cumin (added and stirred) for about 5 minutes each side until crisp, draining it on kitchen paper as you go. Pop it in the fridge, then in the morning slice and toast 4 muffins, then stuff each one with the spiced tofu and slices of tomato. If you are able to eat this hot, you could fry the tofu in the morning; if not, it is just as good cold.

Corn, Carrot and Peanut Tacos

Make a salad with 4 grated carrots, 135g baby corn sliced into discs, and 4 tablespoons peanuts. Stuff your tacos.

Minted Mashed Chickpea and Beetroot Taquitos

Take 8 heaped tablespoons cooked chickpeas and mash them with 2 teaspoon dried mint. Add one finely chopped onion plus salt and pepper to taste, then lay them out on flat wraps. Top with 4 diced baby beets (from the baby beetroot jar) and seal. Roll into tight cigar shapes.

Rolls with Hummus, Lettuce and Grated Carrot

Make the hummus by blending 500g cooked chickpeas with 4 tablespoons olive oil, 2 chopped garlic cloves, the juice of a lemon and salt and pepper to taste. Add a little water if necessary. Grate 2 carrots and mix into your hummus, then spread over your split rolls and top with shredded lettuce before the closing ceremony.

Peanut Butter and Spiced Apple Sandwiches

Sprinkle the slices cut from 2 apples with a light dusting of nutmeg. Spread one slice of bread with the peanut butter and top with the spiced apple. Take the other slice, join and enjoy.

Pixie Ploughman's with Chorizo

Everything in miniature! On each plate arrange some whole washed lettuce leaves topped with cherry tomatoes, cocktail onions, slices of cooked vegan chorizo sausages, baby beetroots and mini breadsticks.

Smashed Teriyaki Chickpeas and Chopped Apple Sandwiches

Take 8 heaped tablespoons chickpeas and mash them with 2 tablespoons teriyaki sauce and mix in a finely chopped onion. Core and chop 2 apples, mix them with the chickpeas, and fill your sandwiches.

Birthday Persian Rock Cakes

These little light cakes are a particular favourite of mine. They are quick, supremely easy to make and are very economical. Sprinkle a classically Persian ingredient into classically English cake mix which has stood the test of time and you have breakfast fit for a birthday.

Ingredients

450g plain flour
2 teaspoons baking powder
¾ teaspoon ground mixed spice
250g margarine, cold from the fridge, diced
2 rounded tablespoons soft brown sugar
200g sultanas
80g tub of pomegranate seeds
3 rounded teaspoons apple sauce
2 tablespoons plant milk, whisked together with a fork pinch of salt

Method

1) Preheat the oven to 200°C/400°F/Gas Mark 6. Grease a baking sheet.

2) Sift the flour, salt and baking powder into a bowl and stir in the mixed spice. Rinse your hands in cold water, dry them, then rub the margarine into the mixture until you have little breadcrumbs. Try just to use the tips of your fingers because you want to keep the marg as cold as possible.

3) Add the sugar, the dried fruit, the pomegranate seeds and the plant milk/apple sauce mixture.

4) Gently stir until everything is just combined, as you would with muffins. If you overmix, you'll end up with tough cakes.

5) Using a tablespoon (serving-spoon size, not the measurement), put 8 rock-like heaps of the mixture onto your baking sheet, making sure you have plenty of room around each cake to allow them to spread.

6) Bake for about 12–15 minutes, until browned. Leave to cool on a wire rack. (The pomegranate seeds get startlingly hot).

7) Serve with birthday candles stuck into them at odd angles. If you happen to come across these candle holders with tiny garden forks, so much the better to shift rocks.

Dinners for Winter, Week Two

1. Fire-Breathing Green Dragon Pie

2. Double Corn Stroganoff with Chilli Rice

3. Italian Movie Night

4. Mini Portobello Mushrooms in
   Cheesy Polenta with Caramelised
   Red Onion and Garlic

5. Squashy Bubble

6. Winter Spiral High Tea

7. Sausages with Rich Onion
   Teriyaki Gravy and Polenta

Shopping List for Dinners for Winter, Week Two

	Prices (£)
Vegetables/Fruit	
759g organic carrots	00.95
spring onions	00.37
1.5 kg organic potatoes	01.39
130g baby corn	00.99
250g chestnut mushrooms	00.95
225g green beans	00.95
spring greens	00.69
mixed chillies	00.57
2 lemons @ 29p each	00.58
red cabbage	00.79
2 garlic bulbs @ 30p each	00.60
250g baby portobello mushrooms	01.25
2 red onions @12p each	00.24
1 pineapple	00.89
1 red pepper	00.60
30g basil	00.52
30g thyme	00.50
6 kiwi.	00.49
Fridge	
vegan margarine	01.20
1 litre plant milk	01.40
2 x 200g extra mature vegan cheddar @ £2 each	04.00
vegan frankfurters	03.50
fresh thyme	00.60
150g Violife Blue	02.99
8 vegetarian sausages (e.g. Cauldron)	02.89
225g vegan cream cheese	02.25

1 500g coconut yoghurt	01.40

Cupboard

275g long grain brown rice	00.99
chopped tomatoes	00.34
1.5kg plain flour	00.45
6 hotdog buns	01.00
1 kg porridge oats	00.75
2 x 300g firm silken tofu @ £1.25 each	02.50
500g fine polenta	00.79
stock cubes	00.35
sundried tomato paste	00.75
balsamic vinegar	01.00
popping corn	01.00
340g pickled beetroot	00.40
280g vegan mayonnaise	02.00
14g Herbes de Provence	00.70
400g cannellini beans	00.85
80g pomegranate seeds	01.00
150g packet of oat cakes	00.59
525g carton of vegan custard	00.90
1 can green lentils	00.55

Freezer

900g frozen sweetcorn.	00.89
TOTAL	**£50.46**

Already accounted for: Dijon mustard, organic onions, olive oil, soy sauce, tomato puree and frozen peas.

Fire-Breathing Green Dragon Pie

This is a hotter version of Red Dragon Pie, made with green lentils instead of aduki beans. Red Dragon pie is so named because in China, where the dragon a potent symbol for many, aduki beans are called "red dragons" because they are little powerhouses of nutrients. Lentils are wholesome too, so I don't think it is too much of a cheek to borrow the symbolism for the title.

Ingredients

1 400g can green lentils
1 tablespoon oil
1 onion, finely chopped
1 bunch spring onions, chopped finely (cut off the root system but leave the green parts on)
4 large carrots, diced finely
2 green chillies, chopped finely
1 teaspoon dried mustard powder
1–2 tablespoons soy sauce; depending on how salty the tinned beans were

2 tablespoons tomato puree
1 teaspoon Herbes de Provence
2 cloves garlic, chopped finely
500ml vegetable stock made from 2 reduced salt veggie cubes and boiling water
500g potatoes, peeled
50g vegan margarine
2 tablespoons plant milk
Serve with broccoli or romanesco

Method

1) Pre-heat oven to gas mark 6/200°C/400°F. Put the water on to boil for the potatoes.

2) Drain and rinse the green lentils (of course you could cook green lentils from scratch; boil 200g washed dried lentils for about 30 minutes until soft – there is no need to pre-soak). Put them in the bowl with the finely chopped garlic and set aside.

3) Heat the oil and fry the onion and chilli for 5 minutes.

4) Add the carrots, fry for 3 minutes, then add the stock. Bring to the boil, add the soy sauce, mustard powder, tomato puree and Herbes de Provence, then simmer for 15 minutes.

5) Add the lentils and garlic, then cook for a further 5 minutes. Transfer to an ovenproof dish.

6) Boil the potatoes for about 20 minutes (hopefully the water will have boiled while the carrots are simmering). When they are tender, mash them with the half the margarine and plant milk, then spread over the lentil mixture. Fork up the potato well, because this will give you lovely crispy bits where the potato is thinnest. Dot the potato with the remaining margarine or little splashes of milk.

7) Cook for 20 minutes or until the top is brown and crispy.

8) It is fun to put a green dragon on top (what do you mean, you haven't got one?) and to make trees from the broccoli or romanesco florets for the dragon to emerge from.

Double Corn Stroganoff with Chilli Rice

This internationally popular recipe really began life as a fusion recipe in the nineteenth century, with the Stroganoff family's French chef adding his own touches to an old Russian recipe, and cooks have been adding their own touches ever since. Here is a version which replaces the beef with corn, and is delicious and satisfying as well as cruelty free.

NB: You can cook the rice the night before if you have time.

Ingredients

300g firm silken tofu
Juice of one lemon
1 clove garlic, chopped finely
1 tin chopped tomatoes, processed
to a puree
1 tablespoon tomato puree
4 tablespoons frozen sweetcorn
1 packet baby corn

1 onion
1tps oil
250g chestnut mushrooms,
quartered
300g brown basmati rice
Red chillies
Pinch (or more to taste) of salt

Method

1) Boil the brown basmati rice for 20–25 minutes, drain thoroughly and leave to cool while you make the stroganoff.

2) Fry the onion until transparent. Deseed and chop 2 red chillies. Set aside.

3) Add the sweetcorn, mushrooms and baby corn and fry for 5 minutes, stirring all the time.

4) Add the tomatoes and tomato puree, bring to the boil, then gently simmer for five minutes.

5) Blend together the silken tofu, lemon juice, garlic and salt. Gradually, add to the stroganoff and heat through gently until completely absorbed.

6) While this is heating, fry the reserved chillies in a tiny amount of oil, add the cool rice, toss thoroughly to combine, and heat through thoroughly.

7) Serve the stroganoff on the rice (unless there are objections) so it can absorb the sumptuous sauce.

Italian Movie Night

Popcorn and hotdogs, the standard American and English film-watching fare, can be a bit insipid. If you are watching a movie at home and want to ramp up the quality and taste, you may want to give your night an Italian mood. A veganised Italian onion sauce and a cannellini bean salad will add flavour to your evening.

Ingredients

Hotdogs with Italian Onion Sauce
4 hotdog buns
4 vegan frankfurters
80g vegan margarine
1 medium onion, chopped very finely
300g silken tofu
1 teaspoon Dijon mustard
8 fresh basil leaves, finely chopped
Salt and pepper to taste

Cheesy Popcorn
Unpopped popcorn

55g vegan mature cheddar, grated
1 tablespoon vegetable or sunflower oil, then 1 more for each subsequent layer

Two Bean Salad
Tin of cannellini beans
2 large carrots
I packet green beans
4 tablespoons olive oil
1 tablespoon Balsamic vinegar
1 teaspoon Dijon mustard

Method

First make the onion sauce to allow time for the flavours to develop.

1)   Melt the margarine on a low light, add the onions and cook them very, very slowly for 15 minutes, using the lowest possible setting. (Brown onions spoil the look and taste of this sauce).

2)   Process the mixture in a food processor until you have a thick puree and allow it to cool, otherwise you'll get a curdled mixture. Scrape the puree into a bowl, using a flexible cake scraper so you get every last drop, then thoroughly blend with the silken tofu. Add the basil.

Then get the popcorn ready:

3)   Pop the popcorn by heating the oil in the bottom on a pan with a lid, then add the unpopped corn in a succession of single layers, removing each batch of popped corn, then adding more oil if need be. As you remove each layer, grate cheese over the top while it is still hot. Set aside to allow the popcorn to absorb the tang of the cheese.

Timing of the salad and frankfurters:

The bean salad soaks up the dressing far better if the cooked green beans still retain some heat, so juggle the cooking of the frankfurters with the boiling of the beans. If you put two pans of water on to boil, you can prepare the salad dressing by mixing the oil, vinegar and mustard; open and drain the cannelloni bean tin and shave ribbons off the carrots using a potato peeler while you are waiting for the water to come to boil.

Then cook the green beans for 15 minutes and add the hotdogs to it. Then all you have to do is split the hotdog buns, add the dogs and serve them with the sauce. Mix the salad ingredients and put the popcorn in pretty containers. If you can find or make the iconic popcorn cornets, so much the better! Serve with your film of choice.

Mini Portobello Mushrooms in Cheesy Polenta with Caramelised Red Onion and Garlic

Polenta needs strong flavouring; in fact, like tofu, it is often a vehicle for its partner(s). It also shares the versatility of tofu and is very cheap (79p for 500g was the cheapest I found) so it is very useful to have some in your store cupboard. As the juicy mushrooms, onions and garlic release their fragrance during cooking, the smell is irresistible. So is the taste.

Ingredients

125g baby Portobello Mushrooms
2 red onions, chopped
4 garlic cloves, chopped
12 tablespoons polenta
625 ml water
1 tablespoon balsamic vinegar mixed in 400ml plant milk
2 teaspoons Dijon mustard

2 teaspoons Herbes de Provence
200g vegan cheese
4 tablespoons previously frozen sweetcorn, spread over a plate to thaw
A pinch of salt good grinding of black pepper

Method

1) Preheat the oven to 190°C/375°F/Gas Mark 5.

2) Wipe the mushrooms with a clean cloth then place them, gills uppermost, on a shallow casserole dish.

3) Sprinkle with salt and pepper and set aside.

4) Caramelise two chopped red onions by frying them very, very slowly, on the lowest possible light, for 10 minutes in a tiny amount of oil and ½ teaspoon sugar; red onions are sweeter than the white ones so you don't need much. Set aside.

5) Pour the water with balsamic vinegar and plant milk into a big saucepan and slowly bring to the boil.

6) Lower the heat and, whisking all the time, gingerly shower in the polenta. A heavy hand will cause lumps, I can say from experience. Simmer for 6–8 minutes until you have a thick sauce.

7) Turn off the heat and stir in the mustard and vegan cheddar until incorporated into the sauce. Mix in the sweetcorn and herbs.

8) Pour the sauce around the mushrooms, scatter with the red onion and garlic, then bake for 25–30 minutes.

Squashy Bubble

Even people who aren't squash fans love this velvety sauce from Italy; combine its richness with the humble Bubble from England and you have a divine mixture of the earthy and the luxurious (as in refined, not expensive).

If you enjoy this sauce, it goes just as well with its authentic partners, gnocchi and pasta. And for Bubble and Squeak fans, this is Bubble lover's paradise.

Ingredients

For the Bubble and Squeak
500g cooked old potatoes, mashed with 55g margarine then cooled
1 large onion, chopped
Good grinding of black pepper
500g spring greens, sliced and steamed until tender
1 teaspoon Dijon mustard
25g margarine
2 cloves garlic
2 tablespoons plant milk

1 heaped tablespoon flour
1 tablespoon oil

For the Butternut Squash Sauce
1 butternut squash
1 clove garlic
25g vegan margarine
1 30g packet cut fresh thyme; save 3 for decoration, then run your forefinger and thumb along the remaining stalks to remove the leaves
1 150ml carton soya/oat cream

Method

1) Melt 25g vegan margarine, then fry the onion until transparent. Add the garlic and fry briefly, until the garlic is tender; as always, avoid burning the garlic.

2) In a big bowl, combine the mashed potato, spring greens, cooked onion, garlic and Dijon mustard.

3) Whip in the plant milk.

4) Shape into patties with clean hands, then roll each patty in the flour to coat. Set aside while you make the sauce:

5) Peel the butternut squash (it is easier to do this with a Y shaped peeler, holding the squash upright), cut into cubes, then steam or boil until tender (about 10–15 minutes).

6) Fry the garlic in a 25g margarine until softened, then tip the butternut squash, thyme leaves and garlic in the food processor and blitz until smooth.

7) Heat the oil in a large frying pan, then fry the patties on both sides until brown.

8) In the meantime, gently heat the butternut squash puree in a saucepan. When it starts to bubble, turn the heat right down, then add the soya cream*. Stir in and heat briefly – for a minute at most.

9) Put a pool of sauce on a large plate, top with the bubble patties and garnish with sprigs of thyme.

*As mentioned elsewhere, you could use Elmlea's plant-based cream, but you would only need half a carton.

WINTER SPIRAL HIGH TEA

Red and Green Chilli Cheese Straws, Oatcakes with Pea Hummus and Red Pepper and Tropical Toffee Eton Mess

Did you know that only female holly bushes have the famous red berries in winter? I wish I'd known this before I bought a holly bush that never provided the blast of colour I was after which is always welcome in the colder months, along with the deep green of evergreens like spiky holly leaves and fir trees. I love the red and green colour combination which I always associate with the winter where I live, so I thought it would be fun to use this as a theme along with the spirals for this season's High Tea. If you want to be woken up from your winter hibernation, these tastes will do it!

Red and Green Chilli Cheese Straws

I have found that vegan cheese doesn't seem to behave the same way as dairy cheese when it comes to baking; you need a lot less marg than the butter used in the traditional recipes, so it's worth bearing this in mind if you want to experiment with veganising recipes in the future. The chillies, cooked in this way, only add a little heat but a lot of their wonderful flavour.

Ingredients

1 green chilli, chopped
1 red chilli, chopped
200g grated vegan Cheddar
60g vegan marg cut into pieces
from the fridge – (weigh and put
it back in)

400g plain flour
Plant milk to bind
Pinch of salt

Method

1) Grease and line 2 baking sheets. Preheat the oven 200°C/400°F/Gas Mark 6.

2) Put the flour and salt into a large bowl, then rub the marg into the flour with your fingertips until you have small breadcrumbs.

3) Stir in the grated cheddar, mix thoroughly, then add just enough milk until the mixture binds into a ball. Lightly flour so you can pick it up in a minute.

4) Flour a chopping board and your rolling pin, roll out your mixture, then cut into 6–8 cm strips, reshaping, re-rolling and cutting scraps as necessary. Lay them out onto your prepared baking sheets, leaving narrow gaps for a little expansion.

5) Take the two ends of each strips between the thumb and forefinger of both hands, then twist in opposite directions as many times as it takes to form a loose or tight corkscrew shape according to your preference.

6) Bake for 15 minutes, remove from the oven, sprinkle on the chilli, press lightly into the mixture with the back of a teaspoon (take care not to touch the hot baking sheet!) then return to the oven for another five minutes.

Oatcakes with Pea Hummus and Red Pepper

Have you ever had Pea Hummus before? I love hummus in all its forms but I particularly love this one – it adds a fresh zing, which is very welcome in the depths of winter.

Ingredients

1 red pepper
3–4 oatcakes per person

Pea Hummus
1 400g tin of chickpeas, drained – reserve the liquid for your meringues

8 tablespoons defrosted, previously frozen peas
1 clove garlic, chopped
1 lemon, juiced
4 tablespoons olive oil
Salt and pepper to taste

Method

1) Whizz all the Pea Hummus ingredients together in a food processor.

2) Turn the red pepper onto its side and slice it laterally. Cut out any fibres and shake out the seeds. Spread the oatcakes with the hummus, then top each one with the red pepper slices, shaping them to form spirals.

Tropical Toffee Eton Mess

Eton Mess involves broken up meringue, but this recipe takes it a step further: the brown sugar meringue pieces actually dissolve into the coconut yoghurt (used instead of the traditional dairy cream) and create a divine toffee flavour. The differing levels of sweetness in this (from the concentrated sweetness in the custard and tropical fruit through to the tempered sweetness of the pomegranate seeds) define, for me, what it is to really, really enjoy your food: the diverse flavours seem to dance on your tongue so your taste buds never get bored.

Ingredients

6 kiwis
80g pomegranate seeds
The liquid from a can of chickpeas (aquafaba) — see Pea Hummus recipe
125g brown sugar

500g coconut yoghurt*
one pineapple, halved and chopped
525g carton vegan custard

Method

1) Start by making the meringue: cut some greaseproof paper to fit 2 baking sheets; on each sheet, draw around 2 dinner plates, grease the baking sheets, then put the paper on the sheets with the pencil circles facing downwards. Preheat the oven to 110°C/225°F/Gas Mark 1/4), then drain the can of chickpeas, put the chickpeas in the fridge for you hummus and whip up the chickpea liquid (also known as aquafaba, if you're new to this) into the traditional snowy peaks. This can take as long as 10 minutes, so if you don't have a freestanding mixer you may need to take little breaks!

2) Sprinkle in the sugar, whisking all the time, then whisk for a further 5 minutes.

3) Spread the mixture over and inside the circles, using the back of a spoon, then bake for 2 hours. (You could prep the pineapple during this time if you wish — see below).

4) Remove the meringues from the oven, allow to cool completely, then peel off the paper. Break into small, penny-sized pieces into a large bowl (so you don't lose bits); it doesn't matter if some pieces are simply powder!

5) Assemble the Eton Mess: peel and core the pineapple, cut it into bite-size chunks, then line the base of your chosen bowl.

6) Top with custard, then sprinkle with the meringue pieces.

7) Peel and slice the kiwi, then push half of them against the side of your bowl.

8) Pour in some coconut yoghurt, then sprinkle on some more meringue pieces.

9) Repeat with more yoghurt and more meringue pieces.

10) Top with another thin layer of yoghurt, then decorate with the remaining kiwi and the pomegranate seeds.

*If you want a richer dessert, you could use Elmlea Double Plant Cream, which whips very well.

Sausages with Rich Onion Teriyaki Gravy and Polenta

This rich onion gravy promotes your dinner from cheap and cheerful to cheap but elegant. I was pleased with the caramelised onion/polenta combination in the Mini Portobello Mushrooms in Cheesy Polenta with Caramelised Red Onion and Garlic recipe, so I thought I'd stick with a good thing. I love sauces such as hoisin, soy or teriyaki in gravy; they enrich the taste without impoverishing you.

Ingredients

Pack of 8 veggie sausages
3 onions, sliced
2 teaspoon Dijon mustard
2 tablespoons teriyaki sauce
2 cloves of garlic, very finely chopped
700ml of veggie stock made with hot water and 2 veggie stock cubes, cooled
2 teaspoons cornflour

12 tablespoons polenta
400ml plant milk
2 tablespoons balsamic vinegar
2 teaspoon Herbes de Provence
4 tablespoons sweetcorn, thawed from previously frozen and allowed to come to room temperature, mixed with 1 finely chopped garlic clove.

Method

1) Turn your oven on to preheat according to the temperature specified on your pack of veggie sausages. While this is happening, make your gravy: very, very slowly fry your onions on the lowest light so that they caramelise (i.e. are soft and brown, and natural sugars are released) for at least 10 minutes. Turn off the heat, then stir the cornflour, garlic, teriyaki sauce and mustard into the veggie stock. Mix meticulously – lumps aren't elegant! Gradually add this to the onions, stirring continuously. Cover and put the sausages in to bake.

2) About five minutes before they are ready, gently reheat the gravy and make the polenta: pour the water with balsamic vinegar and plant milk into a big saucepan and slowly bring to the boil. Lower the heat and, whisking all the time, gingerly shower in the polenta to avoid lumps.

3) Stir in the herbs, sweetcorn and a pinch of salt.

4) Swirl the polenta onto four plates, then top with the sausages and gravy.

Suggestions for Breakfasts and Lunches for Winter, Week Two

BREAKFASTS

Pear Quarters Stuffed with Coconut Yoghurt
and Toast with Peanut Butter

Porridge with Peaches and Nutmeg

Overnight Nutmeg and Pineapple Oats

Beany Muffins with Garlic Spread

Banana and Kiwi Smoothies and Toast with Marmalade

Tomato Hash

Potato Pancakes with Balsamic Tomatoes

LUNCHES

Rolls with Hummus and Finely Chopped Balsamic Onion

Sandwiches with Split Pea Spread and Cucumber

Marinated Tofu, Carrot and Pickled Mooli Rolls

Greek Three Bean and Kiwi Wraps

Jewelled Rice Salad

Wraps with Brown Rice, Broad Beans and Coral Coleslaw

Curried Split Pea Soup with Toast

Shopping List

	Price (£)
432g tin of pineapple chunks	00.80
411g tin of peach slices	00.33
227g tin of pear quarters	00.55
4 toasting muffins	00.39
2 x 4 large brown rolls	00.98
2 x 410g baked beans	00.46
6 fresh kiwis	00.50
1.5kg organic potatoes	01.39
1kg organic Fairtrade bananas	01.19
220g hummus	00.55
8 tortilla wraps	00.89
2 x 250g cherry tomatoes	01.06
400g tin three bean mix	00.55
500g green split peas	00.50
Half a cucumber	00.30
1 small mooli	00.42
396g tofu	01.50
Budget wholemeal bread	00.50
454g orange marmalade	00.27
TOTAL £	**12.13**
DINNERS	**51.79**
TOTAL WITH DINNERS	**63.92**

Already accounted for: Coconut yoghurt, tomato puree, nutmeg, oats, balsamic vinegar, onions, carrots, peas, sweetcorn, broad beans, red cabbage, beetroot and chilli.

Notes on Breakfasts and Lunches for Winter, Week Two

Pear Quarters Stuffed with Coconut Yoghurt
This features first because it uses up the yoghurt left from last week's Goreng Meets Goulash. The drained tinned pears have the perfect scoops for you to fill with yoghurt.

Porridge with Peaches and Nutmeg
A sprinkling of nutmeg to your porridge with chopped tinned peaches is the perfect touch. I like a bit of the juice from the can on my porridge too.

Overnight Nutmeg and Pineapple Oats
You could either use the other half of the pineapple (chopped up) from the High Tea. However, I have factored in a can of pineapple in case you didn't make this. You could use the juice from the can for the soaking if you wish, unless you prefer plant milk.

Beany Muffins with Garlic Spread
If you add a chopped garlic clove to your marg before spreading – (put about 4 teaspoons of margarine in a bowl, mash thoroughly and whisk to make sure all the garlic juice is absorbed too) – it is great spread on hot toasted muffins topped with warmed baked beans.

Banana and Kiwi Smoothies and Toast with Marmalade
Blend 4 kiwis with 4 bananas and a little plant milk. I don't find smoothies keep me full for long – lovely as they are – so I suggest the toast too.

Tomato Hash
Steam 750g cubed potatoes for 15 minutes. Fry two chopped onions in the meantime until translucent. Turn off the heat until the potatoes are ready. When they are, add them to the pan with 2 tablespoons tomato puree and 150g of halved cherry tomatoes. Cook gently until the tomatoes are wilted and the puree is completely mixed in and the potatoes are pinkly crisp on the outside. Add salt and pepper to taste.

Potato Pancakes with Balsamic Tomatoes
Take 500g potatoes and cook until tender (see above). While you are waiting for the potatoes to cook, chop up 150g tomatoes and turn them in some balsamic vinegar. Mash the potatoes thoroughly with some marg, salt and pepper, then add just enough flour to stiffen them a little. Stir in one very finely chopped onion. Shape into even size balls

the size of a ping-pong ball, roll into flat discs on a board spread with flour, then fry until brown on each size. Top each pancake with the tomatoes.

Rolls with Hummus and Finely Chopped Balsamic Onion (start night before).

Chop an onion finely, sprinkle with balsamic vinegar, stir until all is coated, then leave overnight to tenderise. Mix into your hummus when you are making your rolls and enjoy.

Sandwiches with Split Pea Spread and Cucumber

Boil 500g split peas (takes 30–40 minutes) until soft. Divide into half, then set aside 2 heaped tablespoons for the Greek Three Bean and Tomato Salad, and the rest for the soup later on in the week. Mash the rest with a finely chopped onion, half a chopped chilli (reserve the other half in the fridge) 2 teaspoon marg, 1 teaspoon dried mixed herbs and some salt and pepper. Makes a perfect spread for your sandwiches.

Marinated Tofu, Carrot and Pickled Mooli Rolls (start night before).

Mix 2 tablespoons soy sauce with 2 teaspoons soft brown sugar and 1 tablespoon balsamic vinegar. Whisk vigorously. Drain and slice the tofu, pour on the marinade, and leave overnight. Peel the mooli and cut into matchsticks, then cover with balsamic vinegar. Put in a sterilised jar (i.e. wash the jar thoroughly, then put in the oven on a low light for ½ hour on a baking sheet). This pickle will last a few weeks. In the morning, grate two carrots, then make the rolls by layering with tofu, mooli and shreds of carrot.

Greek Three Bean and Kiwi Salad

Chop 2 kiwis and mix with a three-bean mix tin and 100g cooked split peas. Dress with a dressing made from 2 tablespoons olive oil, 1 teaspoon Dijon mustard and 1 tablespoon balsamic vinegar.

Cook 500g rice for today and tomorrow. Put half away in the fridge, then mix with 2 tablespoons each of cooked peas, broad beans and sweetcorn – you can start the water boiling for these when the rice has about ten minutes left to cook. Add a little tomato puree to the hot rice, mix in well, then season with salt and pepper.

Wraps with Brown Rice, Broad Beans and Coral Coleslaw

Remove your prepared brown rice from the fridge (see above) or cook 250g from scratch. While you are waiting for the water to boil for 4 tablespoons frozen broad beans, prepare your coleslaw (see summer lunches for the recipe). Mix your cooked broad beans into the rice, top with the coleslaw, then stuff the wraps.

Curried Split Pea Soup with Toast

Take your reserved split peas (or cook 400g from scratch), mix with two chopped cloves of garlic, then set aside. Cut 250g potatoes into small cubes (the last of the 1.5kg bag), then steam for five minutes. Chop an onion, then fry for two minutes with the chopped half-chilli saved from the sandwiches with split pea spread, or just chop up a new one if you didn't make these. Add the potatoes, fry for another two minutes, then add the garlic-infused split peas and enough water to cover plus another 500ml. Boil until the potatoes are soft, with 1 teaspoon Herbes de Provence and 1 teaspoon dried cumin. Blitz in a food processor, taste, then add salt and pepper to your liking. As you are reheating this soup, make the toast to accompany it.

Dinners for Winter, Week Three

1. Apple and Peanut Gnocchi

2. Hoisin Hotpot

3. Hoisin Heart-Shaped Burgers

4. Pantomime Peas

5. Winter Pie: Picadillo Clasico with a Crust

6. Butter Bean Bourguignon

7. Lasagne with Refried Beans

Shopping List for Dinners for Winter, Week Three

	Prices (£)
Vegetables/Fruit	
1 large aubergine	00.68
packet of 3 x garlic bulbs	00.85
750g organic onions	00.95
500g organic potatoes	01.50
59g organic carrots	00.95
8 apples	00.79
250g chestnut mushrooms	00.95
4 x 200g button mushrooms at 85p each	03.40
one head of celery	00.53
1 packet of 3 mixed peppers	00.92
2 x 30g parsley at 57p	01.14
60g fresh mint	00.60
300g shallots	00.75
one extra garlic bulb	00.30
Fridge	
1 litre plant milk	00.59
200g vegan cheese	02.00
vegan margarine	00.85
375g puff pastry	01.00
Cupboard	
tomato puree	00.37
4 tins chopped tomatoes	01.36
2 x 500g vacuum packed gnocchi at 65p each	01.30
568ml cider	00.85
tomato ketchup	00.55
white rice	00.40
300g tinned butter beans	00.33
500g lasagne sheets	00.39
250g Marmite	02.34

500g sultanas	00.88
green olives in brine	00.59
dried thyme	00.49
bay leaves	00.60
firm silken tofu	01.25
350ml red wine vinegar	00.75
hoisin sauce	01.50
435g tin of refried beans	01.35
1 can green lentils	00.55
capers in brine	01.39
340g crunchy peanut butter	00.65

Freezer

2 x 500g veggie mince at 1.50 each	03.00
340g vegan cocktail sausages	02.00

TOTAL £41.58

Already accounted for: soy sauce, olive oil, paprika, cumin, soft brown sugar, plain flour, mixed herbs and frozen peas

Apple and Peanut Gnocchi

These little Italian dumplings need careful handling as they are much denser than pasta. A very nutty sauce would be far too heavy. This is slightly nutty (aren't we all?) and the tartness of the apple and tomatoes is the perfect foil for the gnocchi.

Ingredients

2 onions, chopped very finely

2 firm apples, peeled, cored and chopped very finely (mixed immediately with the tomato so the acidity stops the apples turning brown) plus 1 to garnish

2 tins chopped tomatoes

2 tablespoons tomato puree

2 tablespoons peanut butter

2 500g packets vacuum-packed gnocchi

1 teaspoon paprika

Method

1) Put the water on to boil for the gnocchi and fry the onion until translucent.

2) Add the tomatoes and apples, tomato puree, paprika and peanut butter, bring to the boil, then simmer the sauce, stirring occasionally, for about 7–10 minutes, until the peanut butter is well incorporated into the sauce and turns a terracotta colour, while you cook the gnocchi according to the packet instructions. The gnocchi only usually takes about five minutes, so keep the lid on the saucepan after draining until the sauce is ready.

3) Mix the gnocchi and sauce together and serve garnished with the apple.

This works well with spaghetti, too.

Hoisin Hotpot

This is a potato lover's homage to Boulangerie Potatoes and Lancashire Hotpot; both dishes give potatoes the treatment they deserve by rendering them soft inside but crispy on the top, courtesy of a tasty gravy bubbling underneath. Hoisin sauce, often used in Chinese cookery, gives a rich, slightly sweet nuance to the gravy; the potatoes lap it up, and so will you.

If you want to make the heart-shaped burgers, double the ingredients featured from Steps 1–4, following the method, then refrigerate half this mixture for tomorrow.

Ingredients

12 medium potatoes, sliced and cooked (boil for approximately 10–15 minutes)
1packet of veggie mince
1 tablespoon hoisin sauce
1 tablespoon soy sauce
2 onions

2 cloves of garlic, chopped finely
1 tablespoon oil
400g button mushrooms, washed and halved
1 tablespoon flour
55g vegan margarine

Method

1) Preheat the oven to 220°C/430°F/Gas Mark 7.

2) Fry the onion in the oil until transparent (about 7 minutes).

3) Add the flour, coat thoroughly, and cook for five minutes, keeping everything moving with your wooden spoon.

4) Add the mince and thoroughly combine it with the floury onion, then mix in the garlic, hoisin and soy sauces. Gradually incorporate 300ml water.

5) Add the mushrooms, then bring to the boil. Turn the heat down and simmer gently for 5 minutes – you don't want the liquid to evaporate.

6) Pour the mixture into a casserole dish, then top with the potatoes in a single, overlapping layer. Dot with the margarine.

7) Allow to bubble, brown and crisp in the oven for 20 minutes, but check after 15.

Hoisin Heart-Shaped Burgers

If you can't make up your mind between a Chinese take-away or a burger, you can save yourself the agonising decision (and your money) and have these instead.

If you began this recipe yesterday, you will already have the mince mixture; simply proceed from Step 4. Otherwise, just follow the recipe as it is here.

Ingredients

1 tablespoon oil
1medium onion, chopped
1 tablespoon flour, plus extra to coat (see below)
1 350g packet veggie mince
1cloves garlic, chopped finely
1 tablespoon hoisin sauce
1 tablespoon soy sauce

Tomato ketchup to bind and to serve
300ml water
8 slices of bread: from each slice, cut a heart
Turn all the trimmings into breadcrumbs (see below)
8 gherkins, cut into fans by making vertical incisions (see photo)

Method

1) Fry the onion in the oil until transparent, for about 7 minutes.

2) Add the flour, coat thoroughly, and cook for 5 minutes, stirring frequently.

3) Add the mince, garlic, soy and hoisin sauces and water, stirring all the time. Bring to the boil, then simmer gently for 15 minutes, until all the water is absorbed by the mince. Allow to cool.

4) Mix in the tomato ketchup and breadcrumbs, then stir until you have a firm (but not stiff) paste; stop adding breadcrumbs if it looks too solid, and pop the residue in the freezer.

5) Put a small 7cm-ish sized heart-shaped mould on a plate covered with flour. Push the mince firmly into the mould, compacting it as much as possible; the more tightly packed it is, the more chance you will have of the burger staying intact. Carefully lift up the mould, then repeat this process seven more times, allowing yourself plenty of space between each burger.

6) Gingerly turn over each burger so that you coat the other sides with flour too.

7) Fry each burger on a low light for about 4 minutes on the first side, then 2 on the other, until the burgers are stiff but not dry.

8) Lightly toast the bread heart shapes. Put one burger on the bread, top with a gherkin, then top with the other slice. Put the other gherkin on the second burger. Serve with tomato ketchup.

Pantomime Peas

(Or a topsy-turvy dinner: Giant Peas with Tiny Sausages in Mediterranean Sauce.)

These are a bit of whimsy, invented after a trip to see 'Jack and the Beanstalk' where they bounced inflatable giant peas into the audience. Sharp-eyed readers will spot they are an equally tasty variation on the Rice Balls with Vegetable Bravas.

Ingredients

349g block firm silken tofu

4 tablespoons frozen peas, thawed

2 tablespoons fresh mint

120 ml water

2 tablespoons fresh parsley

20 green olives in brine, drained and chopped small

1 celery stalk, finely chopped

70g white rice, cooked

Salt to taste (you may not need it, as the olives will taste salty)

2 cloves garlic, chopped finely

1 onion, finely chopped

For the Mediterranean Tomato Sauce: the rest of the olives from the jar (sliced) plus one onion (chopped finely); a tin of chopped tomatoes; two cloves of garlic (chopped) and 2 tablespoons each of olive oil and tomato puree.

Method

1) While the rice is cooling (or start with this if you have already prepared the rice) make a Mediterranean Tomato Sauce: fry the onion in olive oil until softened, then add 2 tablespoons tomato puree followed by a can of chopped tomatoes. Add the sliced olives and cook gently for a further five minutes. Put to one side. *Preheat the oven to 200°C/400°F/Gas Mark 6.*

2) Blend the tofu, water, and coriander until you have a thick paste.

3) In a large bowl, combine the breadcrumbs, parsley, olives, celery, onion, garlic, peas and cooled rice, then add the paste to this mixture and mix really well with a spatula, making sure you reach the bottom and sides of the bowl. Add water a tablespoon at a time because you want a firm, but not sloppy mixture, so add it with caution. Shape the mixture into the balls somewhere between the size of a ping-pong ball and a tennis ball. With luck, it should make about 16 balls, four for each person. Line a baking sheet.

4) Cook for about 15 minutes on your lined baking sheet but check beforehand to make sure it doesn't brown; you want to retain the green colour or the joke will fall flat.

5) While the peas are baking, fry some chipolata sausages and heat up the Mediterranean Tomato Sauce. Serve with the peas when they are ready.

Winter Pie: Picadillo Clasico with a Crust

Just as everyone's Spaghetti Bolognese seems to be that little bit different, both in and out of Italy, every Cuban cook has a preferred way of making the mince dish Picadillo Clasico according to particular tastes (or peccadilloes). I like a lot of capers and sultanas in my veganised version (which uses green lentils instead of mince and the substitution of sultanas instead of raisins to stick within the budget), but you may prefer more olives or peppers. Like most mince dishes, it can take a lot of experimentation, so I gave it two more twists and turned it into a variant of the American Pot Pie, breaking up the crust into stars.

Ingredients

1 tablespoon olive oil
2 medium onions, diced
4 garlic cloves, peeled and chopped finely
1 large red pepper, deseeded and diced
1 400g can of chopped tomatoes
250ml cider
100g olives
3 tablespoons capers
120g sultanas

1 tablespoon red wine vinegar
2 teaspoons dried mixed herbs
1 x 30g packet flat leafed parsley
3 tablespoons tomato puree
1 teaspoon cumin
Salt and pepper to taste
390g can green lentils
320g packet chilled ready-made puff pastry
2 tablespoons plant milk

Method

1) Heat the oil in a non-stick wok and gently fry the onion and red pepper with the dried herbs and cumin until the onions are soft.

2) Add the tomato puree and garlic and cook for another 5 minutes until the garlic is tender.

3) Preheat the oven to Gas Mark 6/200°C/400°F, or whichever time is specified on the puff pastry packet.

4) To the mixture on the stove add the drained and rinsed lentils, cider, tomatoes, olives, capers and sultanas and simmer gently for 20 minutes, stirring occasionally. At the end, stir in the red wine vinegar and add salt and pepper to taste. Stir in the fresh parsley, and allow to cool. After removing the pastry base from the oven, carefully take out the weights and paper, then fill the pie with the cooled Picadillo Clasico mixture.

5) Roll out puff pastry and cut it into stars, or whatever biscuit cutter shape you happen to have. Freeze any remaining for future use.

6) Put the filling in an ovenproof dish, then put the shapes on top.

7) Brush the stars with plant milk, then bake for 20 minutes, or until the pastry is golden brown.

Butter Bean Bourguignon

The traditional red wine is replaced with a cheaper cider, and the beef is substituted by butter beans. The meatiness of the mushrooms and the exuberance of the cider sauce mean that although this may be a pauper's bourguignon in terms of cost, it certainly isn't in terms of depth and richness of flavour, which is achieved by using a large quantity of onions and sweet, baked garlic to infuse the gravy. This full-bodied dish is midpoint between a French cassoulet and an English casserole.

Ingredients

500g of button mushrooms, washed
2 x 400g tins of butter beans
2 large organic carrots, cut into chunks
2 large onions, chopped
800g shallots, peeled and halved
2 sticks celery, chopped
2 teaspooons thyme
4 large bay leaves
500ml bottle cider
55g margarine

2 heads of garlic, halved horizontally
plain flour
½ pt. water, spiked with 1 teaspoon Marmite

For Mashed Potato
2 tablespoons plant milk
55g vegan margarine
750g potatoes (other half of the 1.5–kilo bag)

Method

1) Preheat the oven to Gas Mark 2/150°C/300°F.

2) Melt the margarine and fry the onions very slowly, turning and lifting all the time (you could use oil or water to fry, but the sauce will be less rich).

3) Add the celery, shallots and carrots and fry for another five minutes.

4) Turn off the heat and gradually rain in the flour, stirring continuously.

5) Cook for about 5 minutes, stirring all the time, until the flour starts to turn brown.

6) Turn off the heat and gradually add the spiked water and cider, stirring until you have a smooth sauce.

7) Tip the mixture into a large casserole dish with a lid (or use foil if you haven't got one) and add the mushrooms, butter beans, bay leaves, thyme, cider and garlic and cook for 4 hours. After three hours, remove the garlic heads with a slotted spoon. When they are cool enough to handle, squeeze the softened garlic cloves into the casserole, discarding the rest of the bulbs. About half an hour before the end of the cooking time, prepare the mashed potato by peeling then boiling about 750g potatoes (or more if you prefer, but you'll have to alter the budget) for about 30 minutes until tender, then mash with 55g butter and/or plant milk. (Alternatively leave unpeeled and put through a potato ricer if you are lucky enough to have one).

8) Serve with creamy mashed potato.

NB: If you want this for a day when you are working, make it the evening before and reheat it (20 minutes on Gas Mark 4/170°C/340°F) when you get home. The flavours only develop further.

Lasagne with Refried Beans

Do you find that lasagne is the most accommodating of dishes? Not only can you make it in advance (the day before if you need to), but it will easily adapt itself according to your tastes, fancies or what you have in your purse or cupboard. A basic packet of lasagne is available for pennies (as little as 32p at the time of writing), then you can take it from there: your preferred layers and sauces, your favourite ingredients. In this one, adding Mexican refried beans was a blind but instinctual experiment with a deliciously happy outcome. If you can find a pepper with 4 lobes, the end looks good as the centrepiece (I really must get out more).

Ingredients

1 tin 435g Refried Beans
(Roughly) ten sheets of lasagne — it depends on the size of your dish
1 small aubergine, sliced
1 orange pepper, sliced
1 red pepper, chopped
4 shallots, chopped
1 tablespoon tomato puree
1 tin, chopped tomatoes
1 teaspoon soft brown sugar
½ teaspoon salt
250g chestnut mushrooms, very finely sliced
1 litre plant milk
1 heaped tablespoon plain flour
1 teaspoon Dijon mustard
200g vegan cheese: cut off a slim wedge and grate on smallest holes for the topping; the rest goes into the sauce. Put the grated vegan cheese into a bowl for ease of sprinkling later

1 tablespoon olive oil

Method

1) Preheat the oven to Gas Mark 5/190°C/375°F.

2) Fry the onions in 1 tablespoon oil; keep them moving, and keep the heat low – shallots burn much faster than all the other types of onions.

3) Add the red pepper, sugar, salt, tomatoes and tomato puree. Half fill the tomato tin with water, swill it around, then add that too. Stir well, and cook for five minutes. Add the sliced mushrooms and cook for a further five minutes.

4) Place in the bottom of a lasagne dish. In a single layer, cover this mixture with lasagne sheets. Break some if necessary to fit. Spread the refried beans over this layer. This is a bit fiddly as the mixture is thick; add a little at a time, and spread as you go.

5) Add another single layer of lasagne sheets.

6) Make the vegan cheese sauce: melt the margarine, add the flour and stir vigorously to make a smooth paste. Turn off the heat, then very gradually, drop by drop, add the plant milk, stirring well and making sure your wooden spoon gets to the bottom and sides of your pan. Stir in the mustard.

7) Turn on the heat and stir constantly until you have a thickened, smooth sauce. Add the vegan grated cheese and stir until melted. Pour and spread this over the lasagne sheets. Top with finely grated vegan cheese, as indicated above. It is easier to direct it where you want it to go if you are not grating it directly onto the dish.

8) Fry the aubergine until light brown in other 1 tablespoon oil.

9) Place the aubergine slices on top of the lasagne, then surround each slice with a slice of orange pepper in a corresponding size, to make flowers. The end of the pepper makes a particularly shapely flower, so it looks good in the middle.

10) Bake the lasagne for 30 minutes; if it starts get too brown – (some ovens are temperamental) – cover it with foil until the end of the cooking time.

Suggestions for Breakfasts and Lunches for Winter, Week Three

BREAKFASTS

Banana and Oat Pancakes with Marmalade

Chocolate Porridge

Overnight Mango Oats

Sultana and Hazelnut Loaf Cake

Marmalade on Toast with Crushed Hazelnuts

Ground Rice with Sultanas

Breakfast on a Stick

LUNCHES

Rolls with Sundried Tomato, Sweetcorn and Cucumber

Caramelised Onion Hummus with Grated Carrot Sandwiches

Smoked Tofu, Carrot and Pickled Mooli Rolls

Pomegranate and Edamame Bean Rice Salad Wrap

Rolls with Smoked Tofu, Picked Mooli and Sun-dried Tomatoes

Hoisin Potato, Pea and Sweetcorn Wraps

Leftover Refried Bean Lasagne

Shopping List for Breakfasts and Lunches for Winter, Week Three

2 x 4 large brown rolls	00.98
1.5 kg organic potatoes	01.39
1 kg organic Fairtrade bananas	01.19
170g caramelised onion hummus	00.69
One lemon	00.29
270g apple sauce	00.39
8 tortilla wraps	00.89
285g sun-dried tomatoes	01.75
396g smoked tofu	01.50
Sliced budget wholemeal bread (e.g. Baker's Selection)	00.50
454g orange marmalade	00.27
70g chocolate sprinkles	00.95
Vegan sausages (6)	02.00
80g pomegranate seeds	01.00
115g vegan bacon	02.49
Half cucumber	00.30
120g whole hazelnuts	01.72
500g ground rice	00.99
250g cherry tomatoes	00.53
1 fresh mango	00.74
200g button mushrooms	00.75
120g fresh edamame beans	01.00
250g ready cooked brown basmati rice (e.g. Tilda)	01.00
TOTAL	**£23.31**
DINNERS	**£41.58**
TOTAL WITH DINNERS	**£64.89**

Already accounted for: pickled mooli, carrots, brown sugar, sultanas, sweetcorn, flour, baking powder, peas, sweetcorn and porridge oats.

Notes on Breakfasts and Lunches for Winter, Week Three

Banana and Oat Pancakes (start overnight if the morning's going to be busy)
First of all, blitz 100g oats into fine crumbs (not quite flour) in a food processor (or blender, or stick blender). Add 125 ml plant milk or water, 2 mashed bananas, 2 tablespoons apple sauce and a pinch of salt until the mixture is as smooth as you can possibly get it. Allow to rest for half an hour or overnight. Fry in small circles, like American pancakes; use a tablespoon and drizzle in circles. When bubbles form in the middle on one side and it is browned, flip it over and cook for a few minutes more to brown the other side.

Chocolate Porridge
Add some chocolate sprinkles into each hot porridge bowl and stir in. Delicious!

Overnight Mango Oats (start overnight)
Finely chop the flesh from a large mango (remembering to shave off the lovely juicy bits near the stone) and stir into your overnight oat bowls.

Sultana and Hazelnut Loaf Cake
Please see overleaf.

Marmalade on Toast with Crushed Hazelnuts
Roughly crush 50g hazelnuts (leftover from the loaf cake above) by pulsing in the food processor, then sprinkle on your marmalade.

Ground Rice with Sultanas
Cook according to packet instructions, then sweeten each bowl with a little brown sugar and roughly 2 teaspoons sultanas.

Breakfast on a Stick
Please see overleaf. There is enough potato left over this week from the Hoisin Potato, Pea and Sweetcorn Wraps if you wish to make some fried or steamed potatoes instead of the fried bread.

Smoked Tofu, Carrot and Pickled Mooli Rolls and Rolls with Smoked Tofu, Pickled Mooli and Sun-dried Tomatoes
Use the pickled mooli left over in the fridge from Week Two. Use half of this smoked tofu block for one set of rolls, then keep the rest in its water in a sealed container in the fridge until the day after tomorrow when you'll be ready to use the other half. Grate 2 carrots and chop 4

sun-dried tomatoes. Mix together. (There will be carrots left over from the dinners this week). Mash the tofu onto one side of the roll, then add pickled mooli grated carrots/sundried tomatoes. You may wish to add a little salt or soy sauce.

Pomegranate and Edamame Bean Rice Salad Wrap
Please see overleaf for the rice salad.

Hoisin Potato, *Smoked Tofu, Pea and Sweetcorn Wrap (you may want to make the filling the night before)
Steam 750g cubed organic potatoes for about 15 minutes. After about 10 minutes, cook 4 tablespoons each of frozen peas and sweetcorn. When the potatoes are ready but still hot, stir in 1 teaspoon hoisin sauce. Chop the tofu into cubes, mix with the potatoes, then stir in the peas and sweetcorn. Fill your wraps. This is equally good cold if you need it as a packed lunch.

*This uses the other half of the tofu block from the day before yesterday.

Sultana and Hazelnut Loaf Cake

Ingredients

125g vegan margarine
150g soft brown sugar
1 tablespoon apple sauce
2 very ripe bananas, mashed

190g plain flour mixed with
2 teaspoons baking powder
60ml plant milk
50g whole hazelnuts
50g sultanas

Method

1) Plunge the hazelnuts into very hot water then very cold. The skins should then rub off easily. Roughly break up.

2) Preheat the oven to 170°C/320°F/Gas Mark 3.

3) Grease and line a 2lb loaf tin.

4) Melt the marg and sugar in a saucepan over a low light.

5) Remove from heat then mix in the mashed bananas very thoroughly.

6) Add the apple sauce, flour with baking powder and milk and gently but completely combine. Stir in the hazelnuts and sultanas.

7) Bake for about 35 minutes, or until firm to the touch and a skewer (or uncooked strand of spaghetti) comes out clean.

Breakfast on a Stick

The Full English, kebab style, with two tiny Pan Asian (ha!) touches of soy sauce and adding a pickle to a cooked savoury. You'll need to factor in a packet of kebab sticks if you haven't got enough skewers in the house.

Ingredients

250g button mushrooms
1 tablespoon soy sauce
8 cherry tomatoes
2 pickled onions, halved

4 rashers bacon
4 sausages, sliced
4 slices of bread
Olive oil for the bread

Method

1) Dry fry the mushrooms in a non-stick pan for a minute, then add the soy sauce and fry for another two minutes.

2) Grill or fry the bacon and sausages; when they are nearly done, fry the bread in another pan with olive oil to cook both sides without burning – you'll need to do this in batches so have a large plate with some kitchen paper ready to absorb any extra grease – and cut into triangles.

3) Thread the ingredients onto 4 kebab sticks so that they are evenly distributed, rolling the bacon rashers as you go (e.g. mushroom, sausage, fried bread, bacon, sausage, fried bread, sausage, fried bread, bacon, mushroom, tomato, mushroom, tomato, pickle, fried bread, mushroom).

Edamame and Pomegranate Rice Salad

This is a great filling for a wrap, but because of its festive colours, it could hold its own at a Christmas buffet table too.

Ingredients

250g precooked brown basmati rice

100g tub of fresh pomegranate zest and juice of one lemon

120g fresh edamame beans

2 tablespoons olive oil

A pinch of sugar

Salt and pepper to taste

Method

1) Whisk together the oil, lemon zest and lemon juice, pinch of sugar and seasonings. Set aside.

2) Cook the basmati rice according to packet instructions – they usually require a quick 3 minute stir-fry.

3) Allow to cool to slightly warm or room temperature, then toss in the pomegranate seeds and edamame beans.

Spring Recipes

Dinners for Spring, Week One

1. Roasted Root Vegetables and Classy Cauliflower Puree

2. Spicy Redcurrant and Marinated Tofu Muffins

3. Multicolour Vegetables with Gnocchi

4. Glam Chowder

5. Asparagus Flan with Four Monochrome Salads

6. Vine Tomato Tarts with Minestrone Salad

7. Spring Spiral High Tea: Corn and Red Pepper Sushi; Tamari Dipping Sauce; Radish and Celery Relish with Miso; Chilli Hummus and Cress Pinwheel Sandwiches and Coconut Lime Banoffee Pie

	Prices (£)
Vegetables/Fruit	
1.5kg organic potatoes	01.15
cauliflower	00.75
200g button mushrooms	00.85
220g green beans	00.95
3 x 150g asparagus at 95p each	02.85
1 lemon	00.29
1 aubergine	00.68
3 mixed peppers	00.92
1 lime	00.29
135g baby corn	00.89
160g baby courgettes	01.25
100g loose okra	00.49
225g cherry tomatoes on the vine	01.00
box of cress	00.24
celery	00.55
1 x small red cabbage	00.30
750g organic onions	00.65
500g organic carrots	00.58
mixed chillies	00.50
7 granny smith apples	01.35
100g radishes	00.50
1 banana	00.15
small packet fresh ginger	00.50
Fridge	
1 litre plant milk	00.59
251g carton of vegan cream	00.74
160g marinated tofu pieces	02.00
500ml soya yoghurt	01.00

225 vegan cheddar	02.00
375g ready rolled puff pastry	01.00
250g sunflower margarine	00.85
200g vegan mozzarella	02.00
Cupboard	
soy sauce	00.42
tomato puree	00.37
3 x tins chopped tomatoes at 29p each	00.87
1.5kg plain flour	00.45
170g baking powder	00.49
redcurrant jelly	00.57
cumin	00.49
500g vacuum packed gnocchi	00.65
kidney beans	00.30
chilli peanuts	00.85
3 x tins chickpeas at 33p each	00.99
soft brown sugar	00.69
35ml bottle vanilla essence	00.64
6 x vegetable stock cubes	00.39
525g soya custard	00.87
500g pasta stars	00.85
1 418g tin creamed sweetcorn	01.15
500g pudding rice	00.97
150ml bottle of rice vinegar	01.63
1 400 ml tin full fat coconut milk	00.89
400g uncut white bread	00.75
plain chocolate vermicelli	01.00
11g nori sheets	01.63
250ml olive oil	01.30
Dijon mustard	00.39
349g silken tofu	01.40

95g jar miso	*02.00*
1 x 300g packet of ginger nuts	*00.22*
Freezer	
900g frozen sweetcorn	00.89
Total	**£51.97**

Roasted Root Vegetables with Classy Cauliflower Puree

The title may sound grandiose, but this is more gorgeous than you can possibly imagine, thanks to the makeover you are going to give the vegetables. Organic carrots really are a must here. At the time of writing they tend to cost about 70p per kilo more than the cheapest varieties in most supermarkets. However, you only need about 750g, so for around an extra 50p, you get more colour, more depth of flavour and more nutrients than you would ever get from the false economy of buying watery, flavourless carrots.

Ingredients

750g organic carrots
1 tablespoon olive oil
1 large cauliflower
1 teaspoon sea salt

150ml small pot of oat cream*
100g vegan cheese

Method

1) Preheat the oven to Gas Mark 6/200°C/400°F

2) Top, tail and wash the carrots (no need to peel them).

3) Boil for ten minutes.

4) Put the carrots in a roasting tin and use clean hands to massage in the oil, then put in the oven for 40 minutes.

5) While they are roasting, remove the outer leaves from the cauliflower, break into florets, and steam until tender (anything from 10–20 minutes, depending on the size of the florets).

6) Process into a puree with the sea salt, then pop it into a saucepan with the oat cream.

7) When the carrots are ready, gently heat the puree to incorporate the cream.

8) Arrange a swirling circle of puree on each plate, top with carrots and shave some sliced cheese on top.

*Elmlea are now doing a brilliant plant-based cream if you would like to try that instead.

Spicy Redcurrant and Marinated Tofu Muffins

A quantum leap for the savoury muffin. In this recipe half of a packet of marinated tofu is used (the rest is used in tomorrow's lunch). Of course, you can make your own marinated tofu, but you'll have to allow extra time and be really careful about squeezing out any excess fluid or the muffins will be soggy.

Ingredients

85g vegan margarine, plus extra for greasing the muffin tin

280g plain white flour

2 tablespoons baking powder

4 tablespoons redcurrant jelly

1 red chilli, finely chopped

½ ground cumin

250ml soy yoghurt (about half a large pot)

80g marinated tofu pieces (e.g. Cauldron)

Pinch of salt and a good grinding of pepper

Method

1) Preheat the oven to Gas Mark 6/200°C/400°F. Grease a 12 cup muffin tin; savoury muffins have a tendency to stick to paper cases so it is worth doing this. Melt the vegan margarine and allow to cool but not solidify again.

2) Sift together the flour, baking powder, salt and pepper Stir in the marinated tofu. Mix the redcurrant sauce with the chilli and cumin in a small bowl and set aside.

3) Gently combine the yoghurt and margarine. Make a well in the centre of the spicy flour mixture, then put in the wet ingredients. Stir until *just combined* with a wooden spoon (the golden rule of light muffins which no doubt you have heard many times, but it does work).

4) Spoon half of the mixture into your greased muffin pan, then add a teaspoon of spiced redcurrant jelly to the centre of each one, then spoon in the mixture which remains.

5) Bake in the oven for about 20–25 minutes until well risen and golden. It should bounce back when you press it with a clean finger (but take care because the redcurrant sauce is like molten lava. Press the sponge bit).

6) Leave the muffins to firm up a bit in the tin – about ten minutes – then serve them warm.

Multicolour Vegetables with Gnocchi

My daughter used to refer to gnocchi as 'a naff form of pasta' – (that was edited) – but she changed her mind when I gave her this dish for dinner. Bought gnocchi can be drier and more dense than the homemade variety; it needs to be moistened and lightened with succulent ingredients. These spring vegetables are just the thing.

Ingredients

500g vacuum-packed gnocchi
120g red cabbage, chopped
A bunch of slender asparagus, woody ends removed
300g button mushrooms, halved (usually 2 x 150g packets)

4–6 baby courgettes, chopped into small batons
2 tins chopped tomatoes
1 onion, chopped
2 tablespoons tomato puree
200g vegan mozzarella

Method

1) Preheat the oven to 200°C/400°F/Gas Mark 6.

2) Fry the onion gently in the oil until transparent.

3) Add the courgettes, red cabbage and all but three spears of asparagus and stir-fry for 5 minutes.

4) Add the tomatoes, tomato puree, mushrooms and gnocchi, and cook gently for another five minutes. Grate ¾ of the mozzarella and stir it in.

5) Sprinkle on a pinch of sea salt, stir, and put in an ovenproof dish.

6) Cut the remainder of the mozzarella into abstract or uniform shapes, (whichever makes you happy), arrange them with the asparagus spears in a pattern you like, then bake for 10 minutes.

Glam Chowder

The glamorous silkiness of the creamed sweetcorn and the okra are best achieved if you use really fresh okra so if you can't find it, use frozen. Otherwise it will be more slimy than silky. Chowder is served up in many countries (America, Peru, Bermuda, and the UK); if you want to experiment with a vegan version you can start with the three base points of corn, plant milk and a thickening agent or two, then connect the dots in any way you fancy. Here's one possibility.

Ingredients

2 onions, chopped finely

2 red chillies

1 teaspoon sea salt

1 tablespoon oil

500g potatoes, cut into small cubes

225g green beans, topped, tailed and sliced into 2cm lengths

175g okra, topped (or use frozen) and roughly chopped

1 418g tin creamed sweetcorn

4 heaped tablespoons frozen sweetcorn

250ml water mixed with 2 tablespoons soy sauce

150ml plant milk

100g asparagus

1 teaspoon ground black pepper

Salt and pepper to taste

Method

1) Cut the top off the chillies, slice vertically, deseed them with the tip of your knife, then chop them.

2) Grind them in a pestle and mortar with the oil and the salt to make a paste; the salt helps the grinding process.

3) Tip the chillies in a big pan and fry them with the onions until the latter are tender – you may need to add a drop more oil.

4) Add the potatoes and fry for five minutes, stirring frequently so the potatoes don't catch.

5) Add the water and soy sauce, bring to the boil and simmer gently for ten minutes.

6) In the meantime, put a pan of water on to boil for the asparagus.

7) Add the green beans, okra, creamed sweetcorn and frozen sweetcorn, then bring back to the boil and simmer for another 8 minutes. Add the plant milk and simmer for another 2 minutes.

8) While this is happening, steam or boil the asparagus for ten minutes.

9) Check the vegetables; al dente works for the green vegetables but obviously not for the potatoes, so make sure these are really tender before you serve up.

10) Check the seasoning, adding more if necessary, then transfer to a serving bowl and decorate with the cooked asparagus.

One Filling, Two Flans: Asparagus and Rustic Vine Tomato

Vegan flans (or quiches if you prefer that term) are often made with silken tofu, which produces a beautifully airy savoury custard. If you roll the pastry thinly, you'll be able to have enough for an asparagus flan one day and tomato flans on the next night. It makes it easier to achieve this if you put the pastry in the cases in whichever way they fall for the tomato flans; that way, you don't need to use a lot to fill in all the contours. This filling will be enough for both days – easily – and if you serve your flans with different salads it won't feel like repetition.

Ingredients

1x 500g packet puff pastry
3 cloves garlic, finely chopped
1 onion, finely chopped
1 teaspoon Dijon mustard

100g vegan cheese (half of a 200g packet)
300g silken tofu
About 100g fine, new asparagus
16 cherry tomatoes on the vine

Method

1) Preheat the oven to 200°C/400°F/Gas Mark 6.

2) Cut the pastry down the middle. Roll out half to fit a flan case and other half to fit another flan case or four individual cases – in which case you would obviously have to cut that half into four pieces and shape them into balls before rolling; roll from the middle of the circle, (at regular intervals along the perimeter) to the outside in one direction. You need to do some calculation here; I used a 35 x 12 cm fluted tin for the asparagus flan and 4 round silicone cases with 12cm widths. If my maths is right, that makes a total area of 533.04 cm, so you can use whichever pie plates/cases/dishes you have to hand for your two meals by roughly working out the total area of them.

3) Once your containers are lined, put greaseproof paper on the pastry, top with baking beans (or uncooked pulses/washed stones) as weights and bake for 10 minutes to seal the bottom. Remove from the oven and allow to cool a little before removing the paper and weights.

4) Water fry the onions until translucent.

5) Add the garlic and fry for a further 2 minutes.

6) Blend together the tofu, mustard and cheese then add the onions and garlic.

7) In one flan case, arrange the asparagus spears as you like them.

8) In the other case(s), arrange the tomatoes.

9) Spoon the filling in equal proportions in each flan case. Bake the flans for 15–20 minutes until lightly browned.

10) For tomorrow's tomato flan(s), reheat in the oven for ten minutes at the same temperature.

Four Monochrome Salads and Minestrone Salad with Lemon Dressing

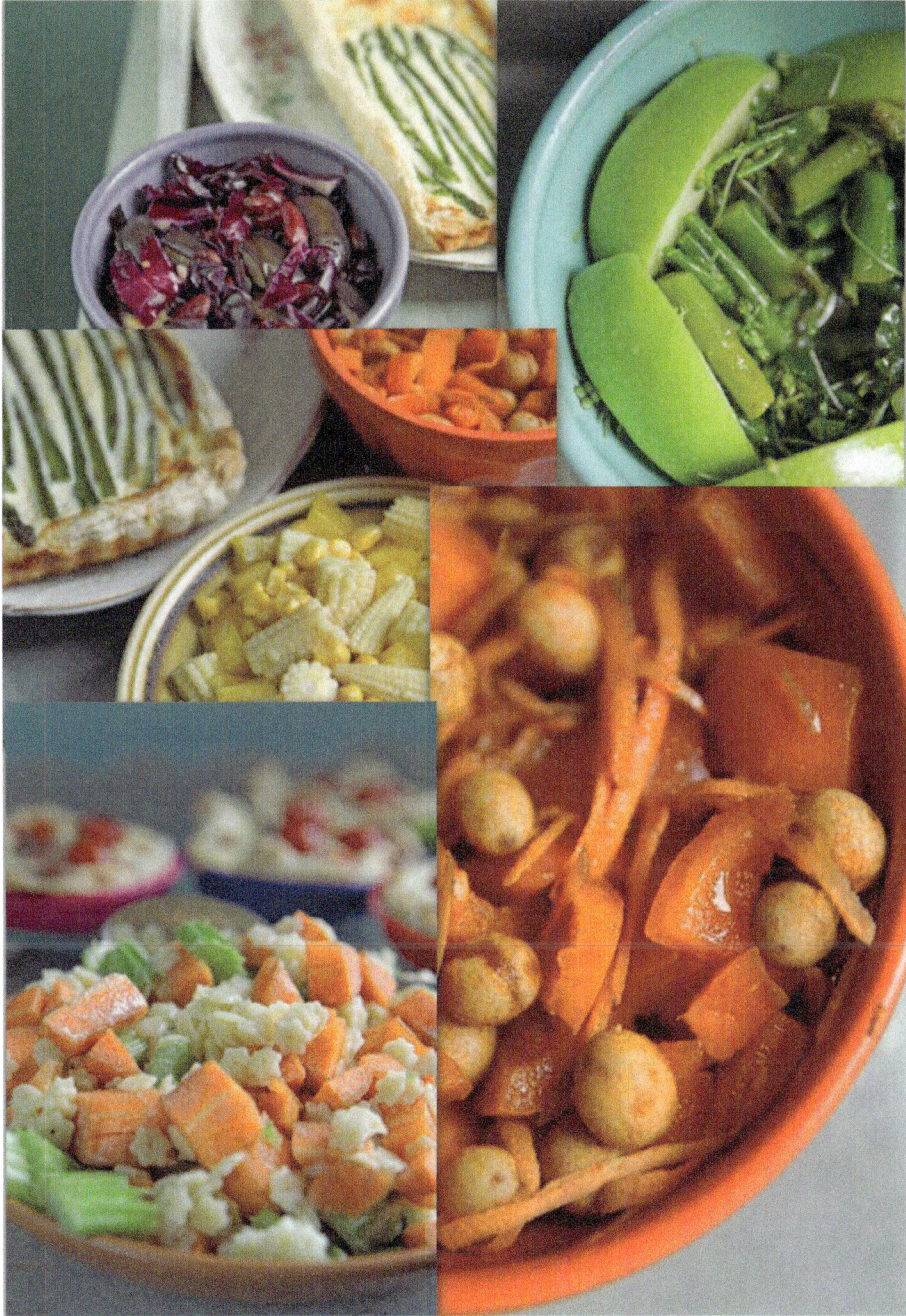

This dressing will be enough for all five salads if you want them to glisten rather than be drenched; obviously you will have to keep some back for the minestrone salad for the following day for the tomato flans. If you make the purple salad first, the aubergine will benefit from some marinating while you make the others to go with the asparagus flan.

Before you start the salads, pop the water on to boil for the green beans.

Dressing
Whisk together the zest and juice of a lemon with one 1 teaspoon Dijon mustard, and 2 tablespoons olive oil.

Purple
Chop and fry a small aubergine in 1 tablespoon oil until tender; combine with a drained can of kidney beans and 50g of chopped red cabbage. Dress immediately and allow to marinate.

Green
Combine one sliced Granny Smith apple with one punnet of mustard and cress and 200g cooked, sliced green beans. Toss immediately in the dressing to stop the apples turning brown.

Yellow
Thaw 2 tablespoons frozen sweetcorn; mix with a pack of baby corn, chopped, and a deseeded and chopped yellow pepper. Dress immediately.

Orange
Grate 2 medium carrots, then mix with some chilli nuts (to taste) and a chopped orange pepper. Dress just before serving to keep the nuts crispy and crunchy.

Minestrone Salad
Mix together 100g (raw weight) of cooked pasta stars (instructions will be on the packet) with 2 chopped medium carrots and 3 stalks of celery.
   Dress the salad as soon as you have drained the pasta.

SPRING SPIRAL HIGH TEA

Corn and Red Pepper Sushi; Ginger Dipping Sauce; Radish and Celery Relish with Miso; Chilli Hummus Pinwheel Sandwiches and Coconut Lime Banoffee Pie

Sandwiches and sushi? Can't get more fusion than that! As this is the season with dormant plants flowering and animals coming out of hibernation, what better way to celebrate this regeneration than awakening the taste buds with vibrant flavours like ginger and chilli? I have to say, this South East Asian take on Banoffee Pie was a big hit with my guests.

Corn and Red Pepper Sushi with Dipping Sauce and Relish

This makes a lot of sushi, so you'll be able have some for tomorrow's lunch. It is a pared down, inauthentic version obviously, but it is so tasty and very therapeutic to make. If you've never used fresh ginger before, you simply cut a piece from a piece of ginger, peel it, then finely chop or grate it. Keep the rest of the unpeeled ginger in the fridge until you use it in the Ginger Dipping Sauce. I have used pudding instead of sushi rice to remain within the budget; the consistency is similar, so it worked very well; such is the power of fusion food.

Ingredients

250g pudding rice
2 tablespoons rice vinegar
Generous pinch of salt

1 red pepper
1 teaspoon freshly chopped ginger
135g packet of baby corn

Method

1)   Put the rice into a saucepan with about 650ml of water. Bring
     to the boil, then immediately turn the heat down to the smallest
     flame, cover, and cook gently for about 15 minutes – but check
     before then that it hasn't boiled dry. If it looks as if it might, add
     boiling water from the kettle. Once the rice is soft, stir in the
     chopped ginger, rice vinegar and salt. Cover the pan again. Allow
     the rice to cool and absorb the flavours.

2)   Cut the pepper into long, thin strips. Cut the baby corn vertically
     twice, so you have slender pieces.

3)   Prepare for the rolling: if you have a sushi mat (you can buy one in
     ASDA for £1.28 at the time of writing), that's great, but if not, you
     can use a sheet of cling film or a flattened clean polythene bag. Lay
     whichever implement flat, then have the rice and vegetables on one
     side and a little bowl of warm water and a cloth on the other. Wash
     your hands and you're ready.

4)   Put a sheet of nori on the mat and spoon about 4 dessertspoons of
     sticky rice on the top. Spread it all over the nori with your fingers,
     leaving a margin of about 1cm all around the edges. Rinse and wipe
     your hands, then change the water.

5)   Dip your finger in the water and draw a line along the edge
     opposite you. Lay the strips of corn and pepper about 1 cm from the
     edge nearest to you, then roll the nori sheet up by gently pushing it

with the mat or polythene. Give the roll a little squeeze when you reach the end, so that the nori sticks. Trim both ends, cut the sushi into 2cm little logs, take a step back and admire your handiwork.

6) Repeat this process until the rice, vegetables and hopefully the nori (but it will keep) are all used up.

Ginger Dipping Sauce
Whisk together thoroughly about 4 tablespoons soy sauce with 1 tablespoon of rice vinegar and 2 tablespoons very finely chopped fresh ginger.

Radish and Celery Relish with Miso
Fairly finely chop two celery stalks and six radishes. Whisk 2 tablespoons rice vinegar in the bowl with 1 teaspoon sugar and 1 tablespoon brown rice miso, then pour over the vegetables.

Chilli Hummus and Cress Pinwheel Sandwiches

1) First make the hummus by processing 1 deseeded and chopped red chilli, 2 tins of chickpeas, 3 tablespoons olive oil, 3 tablespoons water, 2 finely chopped garlic cloves, the juice plus zest of a lemon, salt and pepper until you have a fairly thick puree. If you want it thinner, you could always add a little water and process again.

2) Cut an unsliced loaf of white bread horizontally, then spread the slices with the hummus. Sprinkle on the cress from one box, then roll each slice up. (If you want the spirals to be tighter, roll the bread with a rolling pin first until it is thinner).

Coconut Lime Banoffee Pie

Ingredients

525g carton of vegan custard, such as Alpro (reserve 2 tablespoons to mix in with the coconut cream)

1 banana, sliced thinly

1heaped teaspoon soft brown sugar

1 tin of full fat coconut milk

2 teaspoons vanilla essence

1 lime

2 Teaspoons plain chocolate vermicelli

200g packet of gingernut biscuits (usually vegan; check ingredients)

Method

NB The coconut milk tin and the custard carton need to be kept in the fridge overnight.

3) Carefully remove the peel from the lime with a very sharp knife or potato peeler; set the curls to one side. (You'll be juicing the lime later so you'll need to do this first).

4) Remove the tin of coconut milk from the fridge and spoon the cream into a bowl, leaving about 70ml of the separated liquid in the bottom (this will be about a quarter of the way up the tin). Blitz the biscuits into crumbs in the food processor then squeeze in the juice of one-half of the lime. Re-start the food processor then, keeping the motor running, add the coconut liquid gradually until the mixture starts to clump. Press this into a small pie plate or dish that you intend serving from.

5) Juice the other half of the lime, then whisk it with the soft brown sugar. Whisk this into the custard (remembering to set aside 1 tablespoon), then mix in the sliced banana. Spoon over the biscuit base.

6) Whisk your coconut cream with the vanilla essence and 2 tablespoon custard until it thickens, then gently spread it across the custard layer, fluffing it up as you go. Top with the lime curls and the sprinkles.

Suggestions and Shopping List for Breakfasts and Lunches for Spring, Week One

BREAKFASTS

Orange and Vanilla Porridge

Creamy Coconut Overnight Oats

Mushrooms on Muffins

Banana and Oat Pancakes

Peanut Butter and Banana on Toast

Marmalade Munchies

Three Shades of Orange Crumble

LUNCHES

Japanese Burritos

Spiced Peanut Butter Rolls

Mexican Mediterranean Wraps with Marinated Tofu

Vietnamese Style Potato Pittas

Barbecue Mediterranean Wraps

Red Pepper and Sweetcorn Hummus Sandwiches

Sushi

Shopping List

1 kg porridge oats	00.75
4 toasting muffins	00.39
4 large brown rolls	00.49
6 pitta bread	00.45
one lime	00.29
one lemon	00.29
800g wholemeal bread	00.47
300g mushrooms	00.85
pack of 10 bananas	01.59
500g dried chickpeas	01.15
8 Mediterranean Herb Tortillas	00.90
55g brown sauce	00.29
1 x 340g peanut butter	00.65
1 x 312g mandarins	00.35
Bag of 10 oranges	02.00
2 x 400g tins of kidney beans	00.60
One round lettuce	00.40
454g marmalade	00.27
150g desiccated coconut	00.79
TOTAL	**£12.97**
DINNERS	**£51.97**
TOTAL WITH DINNERS	**£64.94**

Already accounted for: flour, soft brown sugar, plant milk, rice vinegar, soy sauce, redcurrant jelly, ginger, olive oil, celery, apples, peppers, radishes and sweetcorn.

Notes on Breakfasts and Lunches for Spring, Week One

Orange and Vanilla Porridge
Peel and chop 2 oranges. After making your porridge, divide the orange between the 4 bowls, adding ½ teaspoon vanilla essence to each one.

Creamy Coconut Overnight Oats
Make the overnight oats with plant milk and add 2 teaspoons desiccated coconut into each bowl.

Mushrooms on Muffins
Fry some mushrooms in a little oil and 1 tablespoon brown sauce, then tumble over toasted muffins.

Banana and Oat Pancakes
Please see Notes on the Winter breakfasts, Week Three.

Marmalade Munchies (make the night before)
Mix 1 teaspoon desiccated coconut with ½ teaspoon marmalade. Wet your hands slightly, then roll into a little ball. Do this 16 times, then bake in the oven on a baking sheet lined with non-stick paper for 10 minutes at 180°C/350°F/Gas Mark 4.

Allow to cool and serve with a segmented orange each. Best made the night before.

Tri-Orange Crumble (best reserved for a day when you have more time)
Drain a tin of mandarins (reserving juice), then mix them with the chopped segments of 4 oranges. Add 2 teaspoons marmalade and mix well. Rub 110g of fridge-cold vegan margarine into 175g flour, then stir in 80g soft brown sugar and 20g desiccated coconut. Bake at 190°C/375°F/Gas Mark 5 for half an hour, or until crisp.

Japanese Burritos (cook the chickpeas the night before)
Put the contents of your 500g bag of dried chickpeas in a large saucepan with plenty of water to cover and beyond. Bring to the boil, turn the heat off, and let the chickpeas soak for one hour. Drain, put the chickpeas back in the saucepan with another batch of fresh water and bring to the boil. Boil hard for 10 minutes, then reduce the heat and boil (not a rolling boil but not a simmer either) for another 50 minutes until the chickpeas are soft. You will be using these for three recipes: this one, the Mexican Mediterranean Wraps and the Barbecue

Mediterranean Wraps, so divide your cooked chickpeas into 3 and put 2 in sealed containers in the freezer. Label them 2 and 3 and put Box 2 in the fridge, and Box 3 in the freezer (you'll see why below).

For your Japanese Burritos, mix your chickpeas with 1 tablespoon rice vinegar, 2 tablespoons soy sauce and a 2 teaspoon finely chopped ginger. Add 1 chopped pepper (from the bag of peppers for this week's dinners) and some shredded lettuce leaves, then pile into your wraps and seal.

Spiced Peanut Butter and Redcurrant Rolls
Mix 2 teaspoons redcurrant jelly and a pinch of ground nutmeg into 4 tablespoons peanut butter before filling your rolls. Perks it up no end! Sweet things have always legendarily gone well with peanut butter (like the American classic of peanut butter and jam, or peanut butter and banana).

Mexican Mediterranean Wraps with Marinated Tofu
Take your 2 tins of kidney beans and drain them. Take 2 tablespoons chickpeas from your No. 2 container in the fridge, then put the container back as quickly as possible. Wash and chop 2 stalks of celery and mix into the beans, add 4 tablespoons defrosted sweetcorn and the chopped marinated tofu remaining from Day 2's dinner, then dress the whole with one chopped chilli, 2 tablespoons brown sauce mixed with 2 tablespoons tomato puree, and a finely chopped onion. Stuff your Mediterranean Wraps.

Vietnamese Style Potato Pittas (you may wish to cook and marinate the potatoes the night before)
Cube and steam 750g of potatoes (the rest is used is this week's chowder) until tender, which will take about 15 minutes. While they're steaming, make the dressing: chop 1 chilli finely, then mix it with 3 tablespoons olive oil, the juice of a lime, 1 teaspoon finely chopped ginger, 2 finely chopped garlic cloves, 1 tablespoons soft brown sugar. Mix the potatoes with the dressing while still warm. Add 2 tablespoons thawed sweetcorn, 2 chopped radishes and some shredded lettuce, then stuff your pittas.

*Barbecue Mediterranean Wraps
Take your remaining chickpeas from the No. 3 container, then mix them with a quick barbecue sauce made with 2 tablespoons each of soy sauce, tomato puree and brown sauce. Add two chopped Granny Smith apples, 2 chopped stalks of celery and 2 chopped radishes, mix thoroughly, then stuff and seal your wraps.

*Tonight, remember to remove Box 3 of chickpeas from the freezer from tomorrow!

Red Pepper and Sweetcorn Hummus Sandwich

Blend the contents of your No. 3 box of chickpeas with the juice of a lemon, 4 tablespoons olive oil, 2 chopped garlic cloves, one roughly chopped de-seeded red pepper (the final one from the bag of peppers), 1 teaspoon salt and a little water if necessary. Add some chopped thawed sweetcorn before spreading on your sandwiches.

Sushi

Left over from the Spring High Tea.

Dinners for Spring, Week Two

1. Red-Red Speedy Stew with Brown Rice

2. Red-Red Speedy Stew with
   Garlic Pasta Stars

3. Baby Cauliflowers in a Roasted
   Tomato and Coconut Yoghurt Sauce

4. Pasta and Leeks with Japanese Flavours

5. Hash Cooked Two Ways from Many

6. Nut Lovers' Spring Vegetable
   Balinese Casserole with Roasted
   Herbed Sweet Potato Wedges

7. Mushroom and Red Onion Spring Rolls

Shopping List for Dinners for Spring, Week Two

	Prices
Vegetables/Fruit	
750g organic onions	00.95
spring onions	00.37
packet of 3 garlic bulbs	00.85
mixed chillies	00.57
4 large red onions	00.91
2 sweet pointed red peppers	01.45
knob of fresh ginger, weighing about 80g	00.47
3 x 350g cherry tomatoes at 71p each	01.42
shallots	00.71
200g green beans	00.99
135g baby corn	00.99
160g mange tout	00.99
1 kg sweet potatoes	00.94
250g chestnut mushrooms	00.85
4 baby cauliflowers	02.50
175g baby leeks	01.00
2 x 1 kg baby new potatoes at 85p each	01.70
Fridge	
500g soya yoghurt	01.00
vegan frankfurters	03.50
200g filo pastry	01.40
Cupboard	
2 x 400g tins kidney beans	00.60
275g long grain brown rice	00.99
tomato puree	00.37
3 x chopped tomatoes	01.02
turmeric	00.49
cinnamon	00.49

150g flaked almonds	01.39
125g pistachio nuts	01.29
410g tin of aduki beans	00.55
400g tin of black-eyed beans	00.45
500g fusilli lunghi	01.70
150ml bottle mirin	01.79
Vegan Worcestershire sauce (e.g. Chippa) wasabi paste	
4 x 415g tins baked beans	01.29
01.00 (Morrisons) 2.00	
150g desiccated coconut	00.96
90g galangal paste	02.00
30g cardamom pods	00.79
2 x 400ml coconut milk at 80p each	01.60

Freezer

907g frozen peas	00.69
500g packet edamame beans	02.00
TOTAL	**£47.02**

Already accounted for: Dijon mustard, cumin, olive oil, stock cubes, brown sugar, soy sauce, pasta stars.

Red-Red Speedy Stew

A friend of mine, who teaches at a local school, visited their twin school in Ghana and raved about a popular Ghanaian dish, Red-Red, named after the red palm oil and red peppers it contains. Seemingly they put in whatever meat is available, which is often bush meat, and black-eyed beans. Back home, keeping in mind its name, she adapted the dish using canned aduki beans and red kidney beans, for a quick dish after work, and I can confirm it was very moreish indeed. You can easily find red palm oil in supermarkets here, but because I haven't used it in any other recipes, it isn't included it here for economy, so if you want to invest in a bottle you'll need to factor in about another two pounds. Don't add the ginger too early; you'll lose its punch.

Ingredients

1 tin of aduki beans
1 tin of black-eyed beans
1 tin of red kidney beans
2 red onions, sliced thinly
3 cloves garlic, chopped very finely
3 tins of chopped tomatoes
3 tablespoons tomato puree

2 tablespoons oil
2 red chillies, chopped
2 red peppers, chopped
2 veggie stock cubes
2cm cube fresh ginger
Enough brown rice for the people present: allow about 100g per person, depending on appetites.

Method

You'll need a large pot, such as the one used for the Autumn Vegetable Curry. This easily serves 8 people, so you have two choices from many: in this week's menu, it is paired firstly with brown rice, then garlic pasta stars (simply cook a little crushed garlic in a teaspoon melted marg or heat in a little oil, then mix into your cooked pasta), but of course you could serve it Mexican style with tortillas and the trimmings, or with chapattis and mango chutney – whatever suits your wallet or cupboard; it is very amenable.

1) Cook the rice alongside the stew, as brown rice takes a little longer than its white counterpart; put the water on to boil before you begin about 20 minutes beforehand. Pasta usually takes 11 minutes, so you can cook this alongside your sauce.

2) Sauté the onion in the oil until it becomes clear.

3) Throw the chilli and pepper in the pan, then fry until they are starting to soften.

4) Pour in the tomatoes in their juice and add the tomato puree. Stir well, then crumble in the veggie stock cubes. Cook gently for about 5 minutes, then add the garlic.

5) Add the three tins of beans and the ginger, and cook gently for ten minutes.

6) While this is happening, slice two red onions widthways, keeping the layers intact, and fry until lightly browned.

7) If the rice needs more time to cook, make sure this stew doesn't boil; if you only need a few minutes, you can turn it off and put the lid or foil on the saucepan. If you need slightly longer, continue to simmer it very gently; you just need to make sure you don't let all the juice evaporate, but it won't hurt the beans to cook them for longer.

8) Garnish each portion with the red onions and serve.

Baby Cauliflowers in a Roasted Tomato and Coconut Yoghurt Sauce

This dish has a beautiful tangerine-coloured sauce and is perfect for one of the warmer spring days, because it is light but satisfying. Our weather being unpredictable as it is, however, you can vary the accompaniments according to the temperature outside; this week's budget allows for serving it with new potatoes and peas, but you could replace those with something lighter if you prefer.

Ingredients

4 baby cauliflowers (usually sold in packets of two)
500g cherry tomatoes, halved
4 tablespoons vegan coconut yoghurt
2 tablespoons olive oil
1 tablespoon sea salt

Method

1) Preheat the oven to 220°C/425°F/Gas Mark 7. Grease a baking sheet and arrange the tomatoes, cut side up, on it. Drizzle with the rest of the oil and sprinkle with the salt. Roast for half an hour and set aside.

2) Bring a large pot of water to boil and cook the baby cauliflowers for about 10–15 minutes (they vary hugely; once they took 20 minutes) until they are firm but tender.

3) Towards the end of the cooking time (that is when the cauliflowers are slightly al dente but on the cusp of tender), blend the roasted tomatoes with the yoghurt and heat very slowly and gently, only just until the sauce starts to simmer, then pour over the cauliflowers as soon as they are cooked.

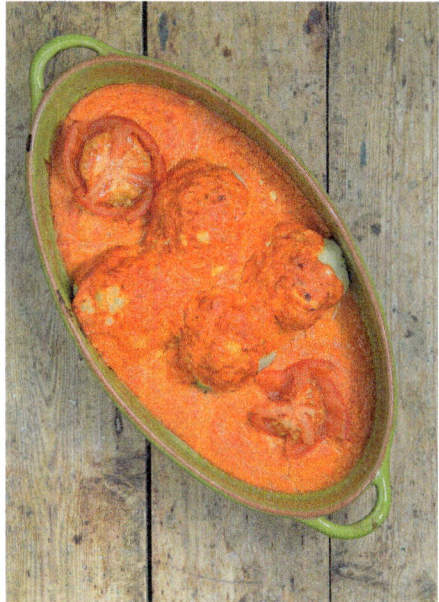

Pasta and Leeks with Japanese Flavours

Sometimes less is more, and a simple noodle dish in Japan with negi, (which is like a large spring onion or a skinny leek, depending on your point of view) is so delicious, it is sometimes served without anything except seasoning. It is also often made with the addition of some meat, such as pork or beef. Spring English baby leeks work as well as negi (and you'd be lucky to find negi here anyway). For the protein, I have used edamame beans; the Japanese flavours are too good to stray from, and the beans and leeks really bring out the best in each other. The fine substitute of fusilli lunghi for noodles is a shapely touch to a simple dish.

Ingredients

340g fusili lunghi
4 baby leeks
150g edamame beans
1 teaspoon Worcestershire sauce
1 tablespoon mirin
1 teaspoon wasabi paste
1 tablespoon light soy sauce
2 teaspoons brown sugar
1 tablespoon olive oil
4 cloves of garlic, finely chopped

Method

1) Take the beans out the freezer and spread them over a plate to thaw.

2) Boil the water for the pasta while you chop the leeks finely and mix the wasabi, vegan Worcestershire sauce, mirin, soy sauce and sugar together in a bowl.

3) When the water comes to the boil, put in the fusilli lunghi for 11–13 minutes.

4) Heat the oil in a wok, then add the leek. Turn down to a low light and fry the leeks for 10 minutes, stirring frequently.

5) Add the garlic and edamame beans and fry for a further 2 minutes.

6) Pour in the sauce, and turn thoroughly until all the vegetables are completely coated.

7) Drain the pasta when it is cooked and toss it with the vegetable sauce.

Hash Cooked Two Ways from Many

The Danish people have Biksemad, the Swedes have Pyttipanna, and the Malaysian people have Bergedil – there are very few countries who don't have their own version of hash, which is essentially frying up leftover meat with potatoes (or rice), vegetables and onions, with or without sauces and spices. The British and Americans are perhaps best known for Corned Beef Hash, which was popular in the Second World War when money and resources were depleted. The Americans even have a day in honour of hash, on 27 September.

It is not usually a dish associated with the warmer months, but it works beautifully with new potatoes. The German and Spanish inspired hashes which follow are not the authentic German Labskaus or the Spanish Picadillo; they simply make use of each country's iconic meats (vegan meats in our case). You could make any hash using this premise – the clue is in the name after all. This is a quick and piquant version which you can make in just over twenty minutes.

Ingredients for either German or Spanish Style Hash

750g new potatoes, washed, skins on

2 tins baked beans

1 tablespoon vegan Worcestershire sauce

Either one packet of vegan frankfurters sliced, or one packet vegan chorizo sausages

One yellow or red pepper, deseeded and chopped

1 red onion, chopped

2 teaspoons Dijon mustard (start with 1 teaspoon then taste, just in case you may find 2 teaspoons too piquant)

Method

1) Cook the new potatoes for 20 minutes or so, until tender.

2) Fry the onion until translucent, then add your sausages of choice and cook until lightly browned and well cooked through.

3) Add the cooked potatoes, mustard, beans and vegan Worcestershire sauce, mix well and heat thoroughly. Alternatively, hold the onions back and scatter them on the top when the dish is assembled.

Other ideas for the faux meat: vegan Polish sausage or vegan cocktail sausages.

Nut Lovers' Spring Vegetable Balinese Casserole with Roasted Herbed Sweet Potato Wedges

Please don't be put off by the long list of ingredients; the first eleven are whizzed into a paste. Balinese food doesn't usually contain so many nuts, nor is it cooked in the oven, but the Balinese flavours are a friend to both and you have the added bonus of a free half hour while it is cooking.

This is a creamy, multi-spiced accolade to the versatility of nuts; three types are cooked three ways in this casserole. The roasted sweet potatoes mop up the delicious juices and provide a jazzy colour contrast.

Ingredients

For the Spring Vegetables in Balinese Sauce

2 green chillies, deseeded and chopped

4 shallots, peeled and roughly chopped

4 garlic cloves, peeled and roughly chopped

2 tablespoons desiccated coconut

40g knob of fresh ginger, peeled and roughly chopped

2 teaspoons galangal paste

6 cardamom pods, peeled and ground (bash them with your pestle to crack the hard skin, remove it, then grind the little seeds)

½ teaspoon turmeric

½ teaspoon cumin

½ teaspoon cinnamon

3 tablespoons olive oil

225g green beans, topped and tailed and cut into 2cm lengths

135g baby corn
160g mange tout
4 tablespoons frozen peas
100g pistachios kernels
2 x 440ml cans coconut milk
100g flaked almonds

For the Roasted Herbed Sweet Potato Wedges
2 large sweet potatoes, scrubbed clean (no need to peel)
2 teaspoon dried thyme
2 tablespoons olive oil

Method

1) Preheat the oven to 200°C/400°F/Gas Mark 6.

2) Whizz the chillies, shallots, garlic, desiccated coconut, turmeric, ginger, galangal paste, cardamom, cumin, cinnamon and olive oil in a food processor until you have a flecked paste.

3) Put the paste in a large wok, then mix in all the vegetables with a wooden spoon. Heat until the paste sizzles, then stir-fry for 3 minutes.

4) Add the coconut milk and pistachio nuts, stir well, bring to the boil and simmer for five minutes.

5) Meanwhile, cut the sweet potatoes into slim wedges and toss in the oil and herbs. Put in a roasting pan in a single layer and put on the top shelf of your preheated oven.

6) Transfer the vegetables and nuts in their sauce from a wok to a lidded casserole dish and cook in the oven for 30 minutes in the rack underneath the sweet potatoes. Just before serving, stir flaked almonds into the sauce.

7) It looks appealing to serve both in little bowls for each diner.

Mushroom and Red Onion Spring Rolls

A mushroom lover's tribute to a Chinese takeaway favourite. If you like Crispy Pancake Rolls and mushrooms, you'll love these to distraction.

Ingredients

500g chestnut mushrooms, washed and halved

2 red onions, chopped fairly finely

200g packet of filo pastry

2 tablespoons soy sauce

1 tablespoon oil for frying

1 tablespoon oil for brushing the rolls

1 pack spring onions – reserve 3 for garnish – chopped finely (including any undamaged leaves of the green part), tails removed

Method

1) Fry the onions in a wok until translucent.

2) Add the mushrooms and soy sauce, then stir-fry until tender. Let this cool.

3) Remove the sheets of filo from the packet and put them under a clean, damp tea towel, otherwise they'll dry up and won't co-operate.

4) Take a sheet of filo, keeping the rest securely under the towel.

5) Add 1 tablespoon of filling, leaving 4 cm perimeter at the top and along the sides.

6) Fold over 4cm pastry at the short end of the rectangle, as if you were making a bed.

7) Fold over one side, then the other. Make sure the filling is secured within.

8) The pastry will still be pliable at this point so you can experiment with more or less filling until all is safely contained. If you overfill and break a sheet don't worry too much – there are usually plenty of sheets to play with (or you could patch it up).

9) Gently roll it up, as if you were making a Swiss roll. Repeat 8 times for 2 rolls per person.

10) Arrange the spring rolls on a greased baking sheet with their seams underneath.

11) Brush each roll lightly with oil, then cook at 220°C/425°F/Gas Mark 7 for roughly 20 minutes until light brown.

12) Wash the spring onions, then slice them vertically in several places about 2cm before you reach the white root. Place in iced water until the strands bend and curl. Lovely with plum sauce, bought or homemade.

NB: If you are lucky enough to live near a Thai or Chinese shop, the squares of filo they sell in packets are much easier to manipulate because they haven't been rolled up like many of the supermarket ones; they are packed flat. They tend to be cheaper too.

Suggestions and Shopping List for Breakfasts and Lunches for Spring, Week Two

BREAKFASTS

Pineapple Porridge

Black Forest Overnight Oats

Pissaladiere on Crumpets

Marmalade and Peanut Butter on Toast.

Banana and Coconut Breakfast Biscuits

Spicy Beans on Muffins

Black Forest Breakfast Crumble

LUNCHES

Herbed Sweet Potatoes and Pea Burritos

Chilli Hummus in Pittas with Edamame Beans

Coconut Rice Salad with Pineapple, Peas and Spring Onions

Peanut Butter, Banana and Beansprout Rolls

Curried Potato, Pea and Edamame Wraps

Chilli Bean, Lettuce and Sweetcorn Wraps

Jacket Potatoes with Garlic and Cumin Mushrooms

Shopping List

	Price (£)
1 kg porridge oats	.75
6 crumpets	.35
4 toasting muffins	.39
4 large brown rolls	.49
6 pitta breads	.45
500g Black Forest Fruit (frozen)	1.59
1 pineapple	.95
2 x 410g baked beans at 23p each	.46
1 kg organic Fair Trade bananas	1.19
1.5 kg organic potatoes	1.39
1 x 340g peanut butter	.65
360g beansprouts	.60
2 x 400g chilli beans at 45p each	.90
8 tortilla wraps	.89
1 round lettuce	.40
400g white mushrooms	1.00
800g wholemeal bread	.50
TOTAL	**£13.45**
DINNERS	**£47.02**
TOTAL WITH DINNERS	**£60.48**

Already accounted for: capers, shallots, garlic, onions, olive oil, sweet potatoes, chilli hummus, pudding rice, coconut, ginger, sweetcorn, peas, edamame beans and cumin.

Notes on Breakfasts and Lunches for Spring, Week Two

Pineapple Porridge
Cut a pineapple in half; put the other half in a sealed box and pop it in the fridge for Day 3's lunch. Remove the hard core and outer skin, then cut into cubes and stir into your hot porridge.

Black Forest Overnight Oats (start overnight, she says stating the obvious)
Stir 250g of frozen Black Forest Fruit into your overnight oats.

Marmalade and Peanut Butter on Toast
A British spin on the Peanut Butter and Jelly (Jam) American invention! Use about 2 teaspoons of each per person. I think it works better if you spread the peanut butter on first.

Banana and Coconut Breakfast Biscuits
Preheat the oven to Gas Mark4/180°C/350°F and grease and line a baking tray. Cream 125g vegan marg with 200g soft brown sugar and 25g of desiccated coconut.

Mix in 2 mashed bananas and 30g rolled oats. Put teaspoons of the mixture on the tray and bake for roughly ten minutes or until the biscuits are golden brown.

Spicy Beans on Muffins
Stir in a pinch of cumin and half a teaspoon of galangal paste as you're warming your beans to pep them up while you're toasting your muffins. I allow ½ tin per person.

Pissaladiere on Crumpets (best reserved for when you have more time)
Please see recipes at the end of these notes.

Black Forest Breakfast Crumble (extra time needed)
Use the remainder of the frozen black forest fruits as your base, then top it with the crumble described in this season's Week One and proceed with that recipe.

Herbed Sweet Potato and Pea Burritos (you may wish to cook the sweet potatoes the night before)

Take 4 sweet potatoes (3 of the packet are used in the Balinese meal) and scrub them clean. Wash and cut your sweet potatoes into wedges. Toss them in 2 tablespoons olive oil and a sprinkling of mixed herbs and bake at 190°C/ 375°F/Gas Mark 6 for 30 minutes in a shallow baking dish, until tender in the middle. Cool slightly, mix with 3 tablespoons peas and stuff your wraps, sealing them burrito-style.

Chilli Hummus in Pittas with Edamame Beans

There will be enough chilli hummus left over from the Spring High Tea at the end of last week to stuff your pittas. Top each pitta with a scattering of thawed previously frozen edamame beans.

Coconut Rice Salad with Pineapple, Peas and Spring Onions

Cook 250g pudding rice (left over from last week's sushi). While it is cooking, peel and core the other half of the pineapple you have left, and chop into rough cubes. Defrost 4 tablespoons frozen peas and top, tail and chop 2 spring onions. While the sushi rice is still warm, add 1 tablespoon rice vinegar and 2 tablespoons soy sauce, a little sugar, 2 teaspoon coconut then the fruit and veg. Mix gently, but well.

Curried Potato, Pea and Edamame Burritos

Cube and steam 750g potatoes for 15 minutes. While still warm, add a pinch of cumin, 4 tablespoons each of defrosted peas and edamame beans and 1 teaspoon finely chopped ginger. Mix well, then stuff your wraps burrito-style.

Chilli Bean, Red Cabbage, Lettuce and Sweetcorn Wraps

Defrost 4 tablespoons frozen sweetcorn, then mix it with 2 drained tins of chilli beans and shredded cabbage. Lay out some wraps and put the mixture on flat, then add some salt, pepper and brown sauce to taste. Top with shredded lettuce, then wrap up.

Peanut Butter, Banana and Beansprout Rolls

Spread your rolls thinly with peanut butter, then top with banana coins and beansprouts (you'll probably use about a quarter of the packet).

Jacket Potatoes with Garlic and Cumin Mushrooms

Please see attached.

Pissaladiere on Crumpets

Pissaladiere is a true border food; a Provencal take on pizza inspired from neighbouring Italy. This is Mecca for onion lovers. The list of ingredients may look absurdly simple but the secret is in the cooking: the onions are cooked very, very slowly which will produce the sweetest onions you will ever taste. Add some contrastingly sharp and salty capers (anchovies are normally used but this is a high performing substitute) and you have a real frugal feast. Crumpets, with all their little holes to soak up the sweet and salty juices, make a perfect base.

Ingredients

1 packet of crumpets (usually six in a packet)
5 medium to large white onions
150g shallots, chopped
4 cloves of garlic, peeled
2 tablespoons of olive oil
4 teaspoon capers (i.e.1 teaspoon per diner), drained

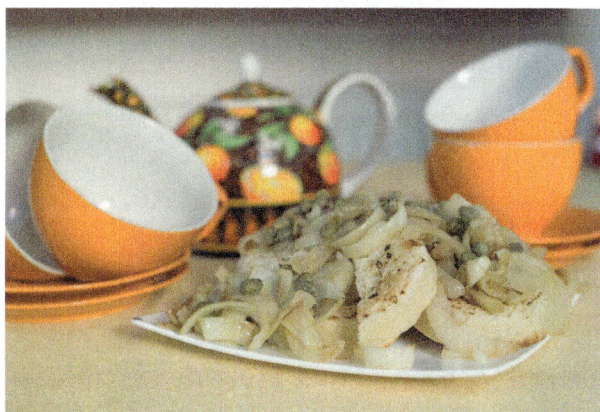

Method

1) Peel, halve and slice the onions thickly (about 4 cm slices), then throw them and the shallots in a wok with the olive oil, turn to coat, then put the hob on at the lowest possible heat. Add the garlic.

2) Cook for 30 minutes, turning the onions about every five minutes so that they don't brown.

3) After 30 minutes, take out the garlic, chop it finely, then put the pan on again for another ten minutes, still on the lowest temperature. (This can all be done in advance and will keep up to three days in the fridge. Simply reheat before serving).

4) Toast the crumpets until they are firm (the time will depend on your toaster/grill). You want them crisp, not soft.

5) Pile the onions onto the crumpets, allowing one and a half crumpets for each diner then top each one with 1 teaspoon capers. Everything needs to be hot and served immediately – soggy crumpets will not cut it!

Jacket Potatoes with Garlic and Cumin Mushrooms

Finding myself at a pub without any vegan dishes, I noticed they had garlic mushrooms on toast and various jacket potato options, so I asked them to combine the two (using oil instead of butter for the mushrooms) and it was surprisingly good! I've added some cumin here because I love it, but really any herb or spice you have knocking around, compliments mushrooms — they're very obliging.

Ingredients

4 medium-large potatoes, depending on what is in your 1.5 kg packet (or two small ones per person)
400g mushrooms

2 cloves garlic, chopped
Oil or margarine to taste
1 onion, chopped
½ teaspoon cumin

Method

1) Preheat the oven to 220°C/425°F/Gas Mark 7. Scrub the potatoes thoroughly, prick them all over with a fork, then wrap in foil.

2) Bake for 1–1¾ hours, depending on size.

3) While they are baking, wash and slice the mushrooms, fry with the chopped onion in the oil or marg very gently until just under tender, then add the garlic and cumin and continue frying until completely tender (but not falling apart). If you cook the mushrooms too quickly, you'll lose a lot of volume, so it is better to go slowly. Reheat gently when the potatoes are ready, then combine the two.

Dinners for Spring, Week Three

1. Baby Cauliflowers in a Comfort Blanket
   with Cumin Flash Fried Apples

2. A Tad Thai

3. Spiral Pasta with Frankfurter
   and Watercress Sauce

4. Romanesco, Thyme and Pepper Paella

5. Especially Grispy Gratin with Garlic
   Mushrooms and Pak Choi

6. Spring Pie: Sausage, Chickpea
   and Leek in Filo

7. Fragrant Sausage Stew with Garlic Mash

Shopping List for Dinners for Spring, Week Three

	Prices (£)
Vegetables/Fruit	
750g organic onions	00.95
packet of 3 garlic bulbs	00.85
1.5 kg organic potatoes	001.15
mixed chillies	00.57
3 limes at 29p each	00.87
one lemon	00.25
fresh coriander	00.69
fresh thyme	00.69
3 mixed peppers	00.92
4 baby cauliflowers	02.50
400g beansprouts	00.63
85g watercress	01.30
a romanesco cauliflower	01.35
500g chestnut mushrooms	01.90
120g baby pak choi	01.00
175g baby leeks	01.00
500g red skinned apples	00.90
Fridge	
vegan margarine	01.20
plant milk	01.20
349g extra firm tofu	01.25
300g *udon noodles	01.49
vegan frankfurters	03.50
200g vegan cheese slices (e.g. Violife)	02.00
Vegan Crème Fraiche (Oat)	01.55
200g Vegan Cheddar	02.00
200g filo pastry	01.30
Cupboard	

soy sauce	00.42
chopped tomatoes x 2	00.68
200g salted peanuts	00.48
800g wholemeal loaf	00.47
150g mixed chopped nuts	01.29
2 tins chickpeas at 33p each	00.66
454g tamarind paste	*01.49*
500g spirali	*01.00*
550g paella rice	*01.10*
smoked paprika	*00.79*
80g tube sundried tomato paste	*00.75*
Freezer	
700g petit pois	00.95
280g vegan chicken pieces	02.50
2x packets 6 vegetarian sausages	
(e.g. Linda McCartney)	*04.00*
TOTAL	**£49.59**

Already accounted for: cumin, shallots, brown sugar, olive oil, galangal paste, plain flour, tomato puree, stock cubes and Dijon mustard.

*'Straight to Wok' variety, which is sometimes refrigerated.

Baby Cauliflowers in A Comfort Blanket with Cumin Flash Fried Apples

Flash fried food is not greasy because it is cooked quickly, at a high temperature; because you shake off any excess margarine before serving, it is not swimming in fat. Bretons often flash fry apples to serve with pancakes; tart apples always enhance anything sweet or subtle, and cauliflower is both. Cumin really intensifies the apple flavour. Baby cauliflowers are also gorgeous with the peanut butter sauce in the Apple and Peanut Gnocchi recipe.

Ingredients

4 red-skinned apples
4 baby cauliflowers
2 teaspoons Dijon mustard
½ litre plant milk
1 heaped tablespoon plain flour
55g vegan margarine for sauce
½–1 teaspoon ground cumin
35g vegan margarine for apples
120g vegan cheddar

Method

1) Steam the cauliflowers whole – (if they are perky and fresh, you don't need to discard the leaves) – for 15–20 minutes, depending on size, until they are tender.

2) Meanwhile, make the sauce: melt 55g of the margarine, add the flour and stir vigorously to make a smooth paste. Beat in the mustard.

3) Turn off the heat, then very gradually, drop by drop, add the plant milk, stirring for all you are worth after each addition. It really does pay to be patient, as I have discovered to my cost after adding a big glug. Turn on the heat and stir constantly until you have a thickened, smooth sauce. Once it starts to simmer, add the vegan cheese and stir until melted.

4) Keep the sauce simmering gently, while you prepare the apples.

5) Melt the other 35g of the margarine, thoroughly stir in the cumin, then fry the apples quickly; about 2 min each side. Lift them out with some tongs, shake them, and drain on kitchen paper.

6) Nestle the cauliflowers close to each other (see photo), pour over the sauce, arrange the freshly cooked apple slices over the mounds and serve the rest on diners' plates.

A Tad Thai

Do you ever fancy a particular dish but don't have all the ingredients? This was born of such a craving, but not the wherewithal, for Pad Thai. So, although, this is only a tad like the original, it still has the classic flavours you'll find in a traditional Pad Thai (sweet, salty and sour), without replicating them. As a dish that respects its roots but has taken on its own persona, it showcases the beauty of fusion food; you can still savour your favourite flavours even if you cannot afford to follow a thoroughbred recipe.

Ingredients

1 large packet bean sprouts
2 tablespoons sunflower oil
2 tablespoons tamarind paste
1 tablespoon galangal paste
1 tablespoon brown sugar
4 shallots, chopped finely
349g extra firm tofu
2 tablespoons peanuts
½ teaspoon chilli flakes
1 chilli, chopped finely

3 cloves very finely chopped garlic
2 tablespoons soy sauce
300g ready prepared Udon noodles (precook or use a 'straight to wok' variety)
30g fresh coriander, chopped, with a few sprigs reserved for garnish
3 limes

Method

1) Cut the tofu into little batons. (This is why you can't use silken tofu). Toss them in the tamarind and soy sauce.

2) Snip the chives into 2 cm lengths, putting a few aside for garnish, plus half of the packet of bean sprouts and a few sprigs of coriander.

3) Fry the shallots in the oil until transparent, then add the chilli and fry for two minutes more. Add all other ingredients, and fry until the bean sprouts have softened but still retain some crunch, and the tofu is firmer.

4) Add the noodles, toss thoroughly, and heat through on a high heat for a minute or so.

5) Serve garnished with the chives, coriander and bean sprouts that you have set aside.

6) Cut the limes into slender wedges lengthways and arrange around the dish; people can then take the amount they wish to squeeze over their portions.

Spirali Pasta with Frankfurter and Watercress Sauce

This gives you a gorgeous double contrast of textures and flavours: crunchy/ smooth dancing with creamy/peppery. Not bad for just over 11 minutes!

Ingredients

1 pot of vegan crème fraiche (e.g. Oatly)

1 packet veggie frankfurters

85g fresh watercress

12oz spirali

Salt and pepper to taste

Method

1) Cook the pasta and frankfurters according to instructions (usually about 11 minutes).

2) While this is happening, put the crème fraiche and watercress in a pan, apply a gentle heat, then cook just until the watercress wilts slightly.

3) Tip in the cooked pasta and frankfurters, then mix everything together.

Romanesco, Thyme and Red Pepper Paella

Romanesco, if you've never tried it, is a brassica which closely resembles cauliflower in taste and is more widely available now, but if you can't find it, you could use cauliflower. However, it is worth seeking it out because it makes such a pretty paella. It is generally thought that paella evolved as a dish for using up leftovers, which is why you usually find it in Spain with chicken, sausage and shellfish. You can find vegan versions of those now, but alternatively you could use the rice as a vehicle for your own fridge's odds and ends and/or favourite vegetables and herbs. A large wok works just as well as a paella pan, but do make sure that you have enough room for a margin which allows for the stock to cook the rice; it should cover it, with about 2cm to spare for reduction in cooking. You may have to slightly reduce the amount of rice you use, but it won't matter because you'll have plenty of veg. If you are particularly hungry, however, you can always cook more on the side and add it later.

Ingredients

1 packet of baby Romanesco, divided into florets

1 30g packet fresh thyme

300g Paella rice

1 red pepper, chopped

1 orange pepper, chopped

4 tablespoons frozen petit pois, spread out on a plate to thaw

300g packet vegan Quorn chicken pieces

1 teaspoon smoked paprika

(About) 800ml stock made with boiling water and 2 vegetable stock cubes

2 medium onions

4 cloves garlic, chopped finely

1 tin chopped tomatoes

2 tablespoons tomato puree

1 teaspoon sea salt

a good grinding of black pepper

1 lemon, cut vertically into eighths

Method

1) Steam the Romanesco florets until tender (anything from 5 to 10 minutes). Put on a plate and cover with foil.

2) Fry the onion until translucent, then add the peppers and fry until softened. Remove the thyme sprigs by running your thumb and forefinger along the stems.

3) Add the stock, salt, pepper, tomatoes, Quorn pieces, smoked paprika, tomato puree, garlic and about 20g of the thyme sprigs to the pan, reserving the rest for decoration.

4) Bring the stock to the boil, then gradually add the rice, stirring it in gently.

5) Simmer the dish for about 15–20 minutes, stirring occasionally, until the rice is soft (but not mushy) and the liquid has reduced. Check regularly – you may need to add more water if there isn't enough to cook the rice. Add the thawed peas and Romanesco. Heat through for about 2–3 minutes. Serve garnished with thyme and surrounded by lemon wedges for diners to squeeze over their paella.

Especially Crispy Gratin with Garlic Mushrooms and Pak Choi

This simple dish is given an upgrade if you crisp the topping twice: once on the hob, then again in the oven. Gratins are loyal frugal friends and the globe offers you endless variations on bread, nut and/or cheese toppings. Panko and pitta breadcrumbs work well, for instance, and any vegan cheese will grace this dish if you like it. Pak Choi may strike you as incongruous – (cheese – vegan or otherwise – isn't widely consumed in China, except in the west, and this is a Chinese vegetable) – but like its relative, celery, it enhances the taste of the cheese.

Ingredients

2 ends of a loaf
100g mixed chopped nuts
Sliced vegan cheese, such as Violife
500g pack of Chestnut Mushrooms
240g pak choi, chopped fairly small
3 cloves of garlic, chopped finely
50g vegan margarine

Method

1) Preheat the oven to Gas Mark 6 then blitz the two ends of the loaf into crumbs in a food processor.

2) Combine with the nuts, then fry with 1 tablespoon of olive oil on a high flame, turning frequently, until the breadcrumbs are crisp but only light, not dark brown. Set aside to cool.

3) Wash the mushrooms, slice them, then fry with the margarine and garlic until the garlic is translucent. Add the chopped pak choi and mix well. Put the mushrooms in a dish which you usually

use to serve 4, top with the vegan cheese slices, making sure the mushrooms are evenly covered, then sprinkle the gratin mixture of nuts and breadcrumbs on top.

4) Cover with foil and bake for 15 minutes.

5) Remove the foil, turn the heat up to Gas Mark 7/220°C/425°F and cook until the gratin is invitingly dark brown – this should only take about 5 minutes so check after then.

Spring Pie: Sausage, Chickpea and Leek in Filo

This mixture makes enough to serve with mash the following day; the accompaniments are so different it is improbable that anyone will notice, but even if they do they're just as unlikely to complain about this appetisingly savoury Southern European blend of ingredients.

Ingredients

8 sheets long filo pastry
55g vegan margarine, melted
Filling (divide by half — except the smoked paprika — if you don't fancy tomorrow's dish)
2 tablespoons olive oil
11 veggie sausages, sliced and fried until brown

1 extra sausage for garnish, sliced, plus 1 teaspoon oil
1 teaspoon smoked paprika
175g baby leeks, topped and tailed, chopped and washed
2 tablespoons sun dried tomato puree
2 tins chickpeas, drained and rinsed

Method

1) Preheat the oven to Gas Mark 6/200°C/400°F.

2) For the filling, fry the leeks in the olive oil until turning translucent, then add the smoked paprika and fry for another minute.

3) Add the rest of the ingredients and stir thoroughly until blended. Set aside half of this mixture for tomorrow.

4) Brush a 7in springform pan with melted vegan margarine, then add the sheets one at a time, overlapping them as you go and painting with melted margarine before each addition.

5) Place them across each other, with a generous margin of pastry hanging over either side. Make sure the bottom of the tin is completely covered, with no gaps.

6) Add the filling with care and spread it across the bottom.

7) Bring up the edges of the pie one by one so that they lie across the filling, brushing each sheet with melted butter before adding another the next one.

8) Cook for 20–30 minutes, until nut brown. A few minutes before the end of the cooking time, fry the sausage slices until brown, then place a ring of sausage discs on the pie as a garnish.

Fragrant Sausage Stew with Garlic Mash

If you rename yesterday's savoury mix for the pie, you are more likely to get away with the repetition, but of course it depends on how culinary minded your fellow diners are! Remove the portion from the fridge at least half an hour before you cook it to allow it to come to room temperature. If you want to cook this independently of the pie, obviously you can follow the instructions given for the filling.

Make garlic mash: boil 800g old potatoes (peeled if not using a ricer) for about 20 minutes until tender, then either mash or put through a ricer.

While still warm, melt 55g vegan margarine and gently fry 2 finely chopped garlic cloves. Mash into potatoes with 1 tablespoon plant milk and mix well. Start gently reheating the stew when you begin mashing/ricing. Serve on or off the mash, depending on preferences.

Suggestions and Shopping List for Breakfasts and Lunches for Spring, Week Three

BREAKFASTS

Vanilla and Cinnamon Porridge

Overnight Nutmeg and Apple Oats

Cheesy Crumpets

Marmalade and Mixed Nuts on Toast

Smoked Paprika Beans on Muffins

Haricot Crepes

Haricot Crepes with Sausage Discs

LUNCHES

Sticky Rice Salad with Sultanas, Mango and Petit Pois

Greek Butter Bean and Edamame Burritos

Sandwiches with Spiced Smashed Chickpeas, Sweetcorn and Onion

Sun Dried Tomato Flavoured Hummus and Lettuce Rolls

Thai Flavoured Three Bean, Lettuce and Petit Pois Wraps

Pistachio and Cherry Salad Wraps

Pastosas

Shopping List

	Price (£)
6 plant-based sausages	01.49
8 apples	00.79
125g pistachio nuts	01.29
270g apple sauce	00.45
6 crumpets	00.35
4 toasting muffins	00.39
4 large brown rolls	00.49
800g wholemeal bread	01.00
4 x 410g baked beans	00.92
500g sultanas	00.88
One lemon	00.29
120g cherries	00.90
8 tortilla wraps	00.89
Round lettuce	00.40
1.5 kg organic potatoes	01.50
250g cherry tomatoes	00.53
2 x 440g tin butter beans at 53p each	00.53
One mango	00.49
400g tin three beans	00.55
500g dried chickpeas	01.15
TOTAL	**£15.28**
DINNERS	**£49.59**
TOTAL WITH DINNERS	**£64.87**

Already accounted for: chick peas, sweetcorn, edamame beans, paella rice, sushi rice, oats, nutmeg, marmalade, vanilla, cinnamon, paella rice, cheese, onions, sun dried tomato paste, tamarind paste, curry paste, ginger paste, olive oil.

Notes on Breakfasts and Lunches for Spring, Week Three

Vanilla and Cinnamon Porridge
A drop of vanilla and a sprinkling of cinnamon to your porridge is a gently spicy touch if you're not a morning person!

Overnight Nutmeg and Apple Oats
If you infuse each bowl of overnight oats with a heaped teaspoon of apple sauce and a pinch of nutmeg, you'll have wonderfully fragrant oats in the morning.

Smoked Paprika Beans on Muffins
Add 1 teaspoon smoked paprika to the two tins of beans as you are warming them and toasting the muffins.

Marmalade and Mixed Nuts on Toast
Sprinkle a few mixed nuts on your marmalade (left over from the gratin this week).

Cheesy Crumpets
Toast one side of the crumpets until firm (there is nothing worse than doughy, floppy crumpets). Place one slice of cheese on each crumpet (left over from the gratin) and grill until the cheese has melted and the crumpets are golden brown.

Haricot Crepes
Please see recipe at the end of these notes.

Sticky Rice Salad with Sultanas, Mango and Petit Pois
Cook 250g paella rice according to the instructions on the packet, then mix in 4 tablespoons each of defrosted petit pots and sultanas. Peel and chop the flesh of a mango and stir it in. Add salt and pepper to taste.

Greek Butter Bean and Edamame Burritos
Drain two tins of butter beans, then mix them with 250 halved cherry tomatoes. Make a dressing of 4 tablespoons olive oil, 2 tablespoons sundried tomato paste, 1 teaspoon Dijon mustard and one finely chopped onion. Add 2 tablespoons edamame beans and mix in gently, spread over your wraps, then roll up like burritos.

Sandwiches with Spiced Smashed Chickpeas and Sweetcorn (need to start the night before unless you have plenty of time)

Take 500g dried chickpeas, put in a pan with plenty of water to cover and beyond, then bring to the boil. Turn off the heat, then allow the chickpeas to soak in the hot water for one hour. Drain, put back in the saucepan and cover with plenty of fresh water again. Boil hard for 10 minutes, then more gently (but not quite simmering) for 50 minutes, until the chickpeas are soft. Drain, then divide into 3: 300g cooked chickpeas for today, another 500g for tomorrow's hummus and 200g for the Thai wraps. Put the 500g and 200g portions in sealed containers in the fridge, labelled, once they are cooled.

Take today's chickpeas and mash them roughly with a potato masher or fork. Add one finely chopped onion, a splash of soy sauce and 1 teaspoon cumin. Put this in your sandwiches with a sprinkling of defrosted sweetcorn for added texture.

Sun Dried Tomato Flavoured Hummus and Lettuce Rolls

Make some hummus with the reserved chickpeas (if making from scratch you will need 250g dry weight of chickpeas): blend the chickpeas with two chopped garlic cloves, the juice of one lemon, 3 tablespoons olive oil, 1 tablespoons sun dried tomato paste, then salt and pepper to taste. Spread these onto your rolls and add some shredded lettuce.

Thai Flavoured Bean, Lettuce and Petit Pois Wraps

Drain your tin of three bean mix, then stir it into the 3 tablespoons of petit pois and your prepared chickpeas. Make a dressing of 2 tablespoons olive oil, ½ teaspoon tamarind paste, 2 chopped cloves of garlic, 1 teaspoon grated ginger (left over from Week 2's dinners) plus salt and pepper to taste. Spread out the dressed beans on flat wraps, top with shredded lettuce, then seal your wraps.

Pistachio and Cherry Salad Wraps

Please see at the end of these Notes for the salad recipe.

Pastosas

Please see at the end of these Notes for the recipe.

Haricot Crepes

(Alright, these are baked bean pancakes.)

These are crispy and tangy and surprisingly tasty. My family loves them, so I sometimes make them for dinner too, adding a chopped red pepper to the pancake batter and serving a salad on the side.

Ingredients

2–4 drops vegan Worcestershire sauce
300ml plant milk
2 tablespoons apple sauce

115g flour
1 tin of baked beans
A little oil for the pan, repeated for each pancake

Method

1) Preheat oven on a low light. Open the tin of baked beans and stir in the Worcestershire sauce with a teaspoon.

2) Make a well in the middle of the flour, add apple sauce and plant milk, then mix to make a paste. Then gradually beat in the milk. Stir in the beans, lifting and gently mixing until your batter turns a beautiful apricot colour.

3) Heat a little oil in a non-stick frying pan, swirl it around the pan, then when it is so hot it is almost smoking, add 2 tablespoons batter, smoothing it quickly with the back of spoon, so that the layer is just a bean's width.

4) Watch as it bubbles away – don't leave it – and when bubbles start to appear in the centre, it is time to turn it over. The easiest way, I think, is to: (a) slide the half-cooked pancake onto a plate (b) tip the pancake, raw side down, back into the pan (c) allow to cook for about 3 minutes, if that; lift the edges gingerly to check it is browned on the other side at frequent intervals.

5) Make a batch by lining a plate with greaseproof paper, placing a pancake on that, then adding another layer of greaseproof paper. Continue in this way, interleaving pancakes and paper and popping the plate in the oven in between additions. (Of course, you could serve the pancakes straight away, but it would mean you couldn't all eat together).

6) When funds allow, these are good with vegan sausages.

Cherry and Pistachio Salad

If you buy the cherries in high season (around May) they won't be expensive, but this salad has a really luxurious feel to it with the succulent fruit and the moreish nuts. It is just lovely, and really needs no dressing.

Ingredients

200g fresh cherries

115g Salt and Pepper Pistachio Nuts

Method

Stone the cherries, shell the nuts and mix thoroughly. Serve immediately.

Pastosas

This is a cross between a pasty and a samosa, invented by a friend and myself after we messed up some samosa pastry because we didn't read the recipe properly. We didn't want to waste the mountain of filling we had prepared for a party, so we quickly made some shortcrust and shaped them into pasties. They all went and our secret was intact. What follows is a scaled down version for a simple lunch.

Ingredients

500g potatoes
4 heaped tablespoons frozen peas
1–2 teaspoons curry paste, depending on taste
225g flour

115g vegan margarine from the fridge
8 tablespoons (or thereabouts) of chilled water plant milk to glaze

Method

1) Cut the potatoes into little cubes, then boil until tender (about 8 minutes).

2) Boil the frozen peas for 2 minutes.

3) Mix both together with the paste. Leave to cool. (If you skip this stage you'll pierce your pastry).

4) Rub the margarine into the flour until it resembles breadcrumbs.

5) Add chilled water a tablespoon at a time, mixing as you go, until you have a smooth dough – use clean hands towards the end to meld it together. Roll out the pastry into 20 cm circles (roughly) and put the mixture into the middle of each one, leaving a 2 cm perimeter for the border. Dip a clean index finger into a cup of water, then moisten both pastry perimeters, taking care not to leave any gaps.

6) Fold the circles to resemble two half-moons, and press the edges together. Brush with plant milk, then bake your two giant pasties on a greased baking tray at Gas Mark 6/200°C/400°F for 20 minutes, or until golden brown.

7) Remove from the oven and slide the giant pasties onto a pastry board. Cut into triangles so that they look like open samosas (see photo).

Dinners for Summer, Week One

1. A Trio of International Salads:
   Danish Root, Japanese Cucumber
   and Greek Tomato

2. Aubergine and Yoghurt in a
   Tangy Tomato Sauce

3. Summer Pie: Ratatouillekopita

4. Giant Couscous with Ratatouille

5. Spaghetti and Mushroom Chow Mein

6. Summer Spiral High Tea: Tex Mex
   Salad, Blue Velvet Cupcakes
   and Savoury 'Ham' Rolls

7. Lentil and Pesto Roast with
   Courgettes and Lemony Beans

Shopping List

Vegetables/Fruit	Prices
550g parsnips	00.59
2 cucumbers at 49p each	00.98
759g organic carrots	00.95
spring onions	00.37
packet of 3 garlic bulbs	00.85
mixed chillies	00.52
80g fresh basil	00.69
80g fresh coriander	00.69
6 medium-large aubergines	03.90
fresh parsley	00.69
2 x packet of 3 mixed peppers at 92p each	01.84
2 x lemons at 25p each	00.50
2 limes at 25p each	00.50
one avocado	00.95
650g budget mushrooms	01.38
600g courgettes	00.74
400g beansprouts	00.65
330g runner beans	01.80
1 kg onions	00.55
4 x 250g tomatoes at 53p each	01.12
125g blueberries	01.29

Fridge	
1 litre soya milk	00.59
250g vegan margarine	00.85
250g sesame seeds (e.g. Cypressa)	01.09
220g filo pastry	01.00
500g vegan coconut yoghurt	01.50
200g vegan cheddar	02.28
100g vegan ham	01.50

Cupboard

tomato puree	00.37
5 tins chopped tomatoes at 29p each	01.45
1.5kg plain flour	00.45
Dijon mustard	00.35
440g tin butter beans	00.33
170g baking powder	00.69
250g cocoa powder	01.69
270g apple sauce	00.37
300g giant couscous	00.59
125g dark chocolate	01.29
500g icing sugar	00.75
150g mirin	01.75
800g wholemeal bread	00.55
150g teriyaki sauce	01.00
250 ml olive oil	01.20
350 ml white wine vinegar	00.75
150g vegan Worcestershire sauce	01.29
18g mixed herbs	00.25
500g spaghetti	00.20
1 kg caster sugar	00.69
500g split red lentils	00.75
280g vegan mayo (e.g. Chippa)	01.00
500g fusilli	00.45
38ml natural blue food colour	00.69
35g vanilla essence	00.75
310g pitted green olives	00.75
vegan pesto (Sacla do one now)	02.00
TOTAL	**£52.76**

A TRIO OF INTERNATIONAL SALADS

Danish Root, Japanese Cucumber and Greek Tomato

If you make this around August, you will get all the vegetables at their finest; cucumber, tomatoes and carrots are at their peak and the parsnip season is beginning again, so you find the sweetest young specimens, not those fibrous ones. A multi-layered salad feast of taste and texture awaits you with no hacking through a vast undergrowth of leaves.

Ingredients for All Salads

Danish Root Salad:

4 courgettes
4 young parsnips
4 young carrots
2 tablespoons vegan mayo
2 finely chopped garlic cloves

Japanese Cucumber Salad:

1 cucumber
2 tablespoons teriyaki sauce
1 tablespoon mirin
1 tablespoon white wine vinegar
2 red chillies
2 teaspoons sesame seeds

Greek Tomato Salad:

440g tin of butterbeans
500g cherry tomatoes, halved
20 basil leaves
4 tablespoons olive oil
1 tablespoon white wine vinegar
1 teaspoon Dijon mustard
Salt and pepper

Danish Root

Slice the courgettes, parsnips and carrots on the diagonal then boil or steam separately until tender. The courgettes should be ready after about 10 minutes and the root vegetables in 15–20 minutes. This is not really the time for al dente, because soft vegetables absorb the mayonnaise much more efficiently. While they are cooking, mix mayonnaise and two finely chopped cloves of garlic in a bowl. Keep the courgettes warm under a lid or foil until the root vegetables are ready, then gently tip them into the bowl with the spiked mayo. Toss gingerly to coat.

Japanese Cucumber Salad
Slice the cucumber, then deseed and chop the red chillies. Whisk teriyaki sauce, mirin and white wine vinegar together in a bowl. Arrange the cucumber slices in an overlapping pattern, pour over the dressing, then scatter the chillies and sesame seeds on top.

Greek Tomato Salad
If you present this salad without pouring on the dressing, the contrast between the colours (bright greens and glowing reds shot through with cream) are much more vivid. Drain and rinse the butterbeans, then combine with the tomatoes and basil. Mix olive oil, white wine vinegar and Dijon mustard together in another bowl, then add salt and pepper to taste. Serve on the side.

Aubergine and Yoghurt in a Tangy Tomato Sauce

I have adapted this recipe from an Afghan friend so that I could have it all year round, using tinned tomatoes instead of fresh and adding vegan Worcestershire sauce to bring out their tanginess. Of course, you can use fresh tomatoes, which are cheap at this time of year. It is not worth using watery, tasteless out of season tomatoes for the rest of the year – tinned are your best bet. He said he would serve it with meat, but in the interests of both veganism and thrift I honestly think it is scrumptious enough to present without it – you will not go short of protein, because of the yoghurt, and aubergine is a 'meaty' sort of vegetable so you won't go short of texture either. This is another one of those recipes that combine cold with hot; scientifically, I cannot explain why this is, but the cool yoghurt and the warm aubergine are a spa for the taste buds.

Ingredients

2 large aubergines, sliced
4 tablespoons olive oil
1 500g pot vegan coconut yoghurt
2 medium onions
2 tins chopped tomatoes
2 tablespoons tomato puree
2 cloves garlic
1 teaspoon vegan Worcestershire sauce

Method

1) Preheat the oven to Gas Mark 2/150°C/300°F (just to keep the aubergine warm). Prepare two large plates by lining them with kitchen paper.

2) Fry the aubergine slices on both sides in batches, adding sufficient oil as you go, until they are golden on both sides. Drain on the plates lined with kitchen paper, then cover them with foil and keep warm in the oven.

3) Make the tomato sauce by frying the onion until transparent, then add the tomatoes, garlic, tomato puree and Worcestershire sauce. Bring to a boil then simmer gently for five minutes. Keep simmering while you remove the aubergines from the oven, then layer up two small platters, or one large one, with yoghurt, aubergine, tomato sauce, and then again with yoghurt, aubergine and tomato sauce (see photo).

The Versatility of Ratatouille

Ratatouille is the culinary equivalent of a well-mannered guest; you can take it anywhere. It benefits from a long slow cook and tastes better after a day's keeping, so you will get the best bang for your buck if you make a huge pot and serve it in different ways because its ingredients are cheap and plentiful in the summer. What follows will give you enough to put in a pie one day, and serve with couscous the next.

Ingredients

5 tablespoons olive oil

4 onions, chopped

4 cloves garlic, peeled and chopped

4 red peppers, deseeded (including the white part) and roughly chopped

500g aubergines, roughly cubed – the weight doesn't have to be precise though; just work on the premise of using three medium aubergines

4 courgettes, roughly chopped; reserve a few slices if making the pie later

3 tins chopped tomatoes

1 red chilli (or more if you like a bigger kick)

500ml water

4 tablespoons tomato puree

2 teaspoon dried mixed herbs

30g (ish) pack of flat leaf parsley

1sp sea salt

Freshly ground black pepper

Small jar (about 330–340g) of pitted green olives in brine, drained and rinsed – all supermarkets sell a cheap pot or jar, ranging from 45p at ALDI to about £1 at the higher end.

Method

1) Fry the onions in 1 tablespoon of olive oil until they turn a translucent pink colour.

2) Add the peppers, courgettes, aubergines and garlic and fry gently for another five minutes, taking care that the garlic doesn't burn.

3) Add all the rest of the ingredients, except the remaining olive oil, bring to the boil, then summer for at least an hour, stirring occasionally. Longer won't hurt it, but obviously don't let it boil dry.

4) Stir in the remaining olive oil, taste, then add salt and pepper to suit you.

Summer Pie: Ratatouillekopita

'Koptita' means 'pie' in Greek – perhaps the most famous example is Spanakopita, spinach pie. But we all know how adaptable filo pastry is, so here is a ratatouille pie.

Ingredients

Enough ratatouille to fill a 7in springform tin (drain off any excess liquid; you want a moist but firm mixture, otherwise your pie will leak)

8 sheets long filo pastry, plus a spare one for garnish
30g vegan margarine, melted (or a spritz of oil if you have a spray bottle)
Half a courgette for garnish

Method

1) Preheat the oven to Gas Mark 7/220°C/425°F.

2) Brush a 20cm springform pan with melted margarine/short sprays of oil, then add the sheets one at a time, overlapping them as you go and painting with melted margarine/light sprays of oil before each addition. Place them across each other, with a generous margin of pastry hanging over either side. Make sure the bottom of the tin is completely covered, with no gaps.

3) Add the ratatouille filling with care and spread it across the bottom.

4) Bring up the edges of pie one by one so that they lie across the filling, brushing each sheet with melted marg (or lightly spray with oil) before adding another the next one. Cut out a few pastry flowers to garnish your pie, and brush these with melted marg/ spritz of oil too.

5) Cook for 20–30 minutes, until nut brown. Towards the end of the cooking time, slice and fry half a courgette to decorate the edge of your pie.

Giant Couscous with Ratatouille

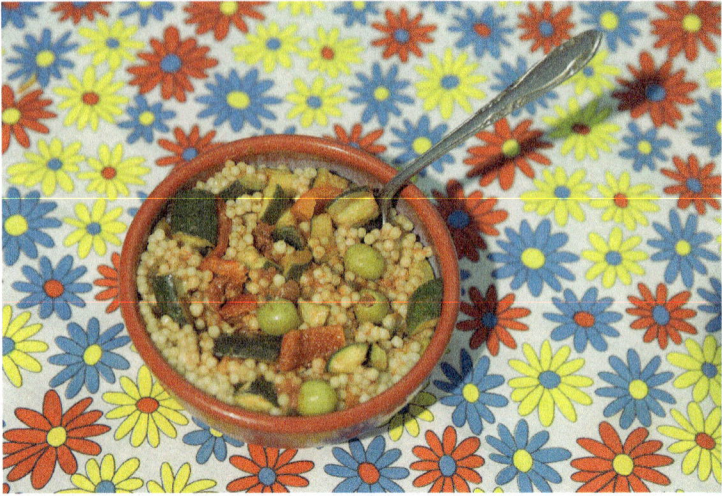

Couscous is as popular in France as Indian restaurant food is here (both sadly beginning with colonisation; Algeria in France's case). It is almost as commonly cooked in France as it is in North Africa. As far as I know, however, although they serve it with a vegetable or meat stew Berber-style, they don't usually fuse French and African and serve it with the famous French country stew, ratatouille. It must be only a matter of time though, because the couscous soaks up the flavour and sauce of the ratatouille without losing its own texture, creating that rare combination of light but satisfying eating.

Ingredients

1 portion of ratatouille, reserved from yesterday's recipe. Remove from the fridge and allow to come to room temperature. (If you didn't cook this, follow the ratatouille recipe, but halve the ingredients).

250g giant couscous (ordinary couscous doesn't affect the taste, but the texture and look is improved with giant couscous).

30g vegan margarine

Method

1) Boil the giant couscous for 6–8 minutes, or according to the instructions on the packet.

2) While this is simmering, reheat the ratatouille gently, until bubbling.

3) Fork the marg into the cooked couscous, then mix with the ratatouille.

4) Serve with some pistachio nuts on the side.

Spaghetti and Mushroom Chow Mein

Cheap spaghetti is a good alternative to noodles if money is really tight and you won't spoil the texture of this classic by adding a fusion ingredient.

Ingredients

1 red pepper, chopped
1 bunch of spring onions, sliced
500g chestnut mushrooms
*1 360g bag bean sprouts
340g spaghetti
1 teaspoon flour

1 tablespoon vegan Worcestershire sauce
2 tablespoons soy sauce
2 cloves garlic
1 teaspoon sugar
1 tablespoons olive oil

Method

1) Mix together the flour, soy sauce, garlic, sugar and vegan Worcestershire sauce vigorously. Pour over the mushrooms and set aside for half an hour (or the night before if you wish). Boil the spaghetti for one minute less than the packet instructions advise.

2) Lightly fry the spring onions for two minutes in the wok, followed by the red pepper for another two minutes, then finally add the mushrooms in their marinade.

3) Add the spaghetti and the bean sprouts, and heat until the bean sprouts are cooked but retain some crunch; this should only take about a minute.

*If following this week's lunch menus, put 60g to one side. 300g will be plenty in your chow mein, never fear!

SUMMER SPIRAL HIGH TEA

Tex Mex Salad, Blue Velvet Cupcakes and Vegan Ham Rolls

In this season's high tea, we have spiral shaped pasta in the salad and icing piped in an upward spiral on the cakes. Of course I also give it the fusion treatment: a Tex Mex salad with lime and Blue Velvet cakes with blueberries, inspired by their famous American red counterparts. Complete your tea by spreading slices of vegan ham with vegan mayo and a dab of mustard into, yep, a spiral, for refreshingly gorgeous summer flavours.

Tex Mex Salad

Pasta salads can be leaden and gelatinous, but if you use warm pasta, or small pasta, it is so much more appealing in my view. This is a fresh tasting salad which doesn't have oil in the dressing, only the natural oil in the avocado. The light zing of the lime juice is perfect in a summer salad.

Ingredients

1 ripe avocado
1 red pepper
200g cherry tomatoes
80g coriander

100g fusilli bucati (the corkscrew style pasta)
2 limes

Method

1) Squeeze 2 limes and set aside. If you can find really small tomatoes, leave them whole. If not, half them, then roughly chop the pepper then toss in the juice of one and a half limes, reserving the remaining half for decoration.

2) Boil the pasta according to the instructions on the packet (usually 11 minutes), then mix it in while still hot so it absorbs the taste of the lime juice.

3) Squeeze the final lime half, then peel and chop the avocado and sprinkle it with the lime juice to prevent it going brown. Mix it in with the salad. Arrange the lime slices around the edge of the bowl and put the pasta salad in the middle. Roughly chop the coriander and scatter it over the salad. The pasta should now be pleasantly warm.

Blue Velvet Cupcakes

Making the icing soft as opposed to stiff will give you the effect of gently lapping waves.

Ingredients

Cakes:
65g cocoa power
2 teaspoon baking powder
½ teaspoon salt
300 ml plant milk
1 teaspoon vinegar
1 teaspoon vanilla essence
115g vegan margarine
170g sugar

100g blueberries

Icing and Decoration:
375g plain flour
340g vegan marg
1 teaspoon vanilla essence
170g icing sugar, sifted
1 tablespoon blue food colouring
125g dark chocolate

Method

1) Preheat the oven to 180°C/350°F/Gas Mark 4. Put 15 stiff muffin cases on a baking sheet (you may need a second one).

2) In one bowl, sift together the flour, cocoa powder, baking powder and salt.

3) In a measuring jug, gently whisk the plant milk, food colouring, vinegar and vanilla together.

4) With an electric mixer, beat the marg and sugar together in a large bowl until you have a pale colour.

5) Then alternately add the wet and dry ingredients, beginning and ending with the dry, beating on the lowest setting, until everything is combined. Make sure you get any rogue flour from the bottom of the bowl (she says from experience).

6) Stir in the blueberries.

7) Spoon out the batter into the muffin cases. (Several cookery writers swear by ice cream scoops for dishing out even-sized proportions and I have to say I agree. You can get very cheap plastic ones).

8) Bake for 25 to 30 minutes, until a skewer or cake tester comes out clean. Cool completely before you begin icing.

9) When you are ready, mix together the marg and vanilla. Beat in the icing sugar and mix until well combined and pipe-able.

10) Put into a large icing bag fitted with a small round nozzle. Starting in the middle, pipe the icing in a wavy spiral towards the edge, making sure each new circle touches the previous one so the surface of each cake is completely covered. On 4 of the cakes, either sprinkle with grated chocolate or splash out on a seahorse mould. You can find silicone as little as £1.28 on the internet, so if this idea appeals to you and you want to stick within this week's budget, you could omit the mirin on the Japanese Cucumber Salad on Day One, and it will still be delicious.

Lentil and Pesto Roast with Courgettes and Lemony Beans

This makes a good-sized portion for an otherwise traditionally British family roast and is equally tasty cold the next day if any slices are left over. Pesto enhances so many dishes, not just pasta or the ubiquitous panini, as it is both moist and flavourful. A jar of this time-honoured Italian sauce in the cupboard helps to stretch the pennies, because it also keeps well in the fridge once it has been opened.

Ingredients

4 heaped teaspoons vegan pesto
250g split red lentils
1 red onion, chopped and fried until translucent (drain well)
85–115g breadcrumbs
115g vegan mature cheddar, grated

2 garlic cloves crushed with
1 teaspoon sea salt
340g runner (or similar) beans
1 lemon
2 large courgettes

Method

1) Preheat the oven to 180°/350°/Gas Mark 4 and thoroughly grease a large loaf tin or a ring tin if you have one.

2) If you are using a non-stick metal pan, it is still prudent to line the bottom of the pan with greaseproof paper as the loaf can stick in the corners, however carefully you grease them.

3) Wash the lentils, cover them with water, leaving about 2 cm to spare at the top, then bring to the boil, and turn down to a gentler boil, but not a simmer. They will have softened in about 15–20 minutes but check after 15.

4) Do keep checking your lentils by stroking the bottom of the pan with a wooden spoon; if they look at all in danger of boiling dry or you find some stuck lentils, top up with water just boiled from the kettle.

5) When the lentils are soft, drain them and mix with pesto, vegan cheddar, garlic and salt into a large bowl. Add the breadcrumbs gradually until you have a soft but firm mixture. It shouldn't feel too 'solid'. Pack this mixture into your prepared loaf pan and bake for about 40 minutes, until the loaf is firm.

6) After about 15 minutes into the cooking time, put a pan of water on to boil. Once boiled, cook the runner beans very gently until tender – probably 15 minutes at most.

7) Slice the courgettes, then water fry them in a non-stick pan. This should take about 10 minutes, so start them about 5 minutes after you have started the beans.

8) After you have turned out the roast, tumble the green beans in the middle (or alongside), then finely grate lemon zest over them. While still hot, squeeze out one half of the lemon (serve the other half with some water at dinner).

9) Arrange the courgette slices around the edge.

Suggestions and Shopping List for Breakfasts and Lunches for Summer, Week One

BREAKFASTS

Cornflakes with Kiwi

Herbed Tomatoes on Toast

Wheat Biscuits with Cinnamon Apples

Cornflakes with Peach Slices

Muffins with Celery and Peanut Butter

Toast with Cinnamon Spiced Marmalade

Pitta bread with Teriyaki Mushrooms and Cannellini Beans

LUNCHES

Wholemeal Wraps with Tomato, Beansprout and Garlic

Rice Rolls with Peanut Butter and Sweetcorn

Tacos with Rice, Sliced Olives and Kiwi

Rolls with Finely Chopped Spring Onion and Hummus

Pittas with Teriyaki Celery and Peanut Sweetcorn

Rice Rolls with Red Lentil Spread

Leftover Roast with Herbed Rice Salad

Shopping List

4 muffins	00.39
2 x 6 pitta bread at 42p each	00.84
6 tomatoes	00.59
200g button mushrooms	00.75
8 large brown rolls at 45p for four	00.90
400g tin cannellini beans	00.33
200g tub of hummus	00.59
8 brown wraps	00.75
One head of celery	00.53
340g peanut butter	00.65
800g loaf brown bread	00.50
500g own brand cornflakes	00.38
2 x 326g tinned sweetcorn at 39p each	00.78
35g cinnamon	00.49
24 wheat biscuits	00.69
8 small apples	00.79
6 kiwis	00.49
454g marmalade	00.27
250g cherry tomatoes	00.53
1 kg long grain rice	00.40
123g peach slices in juice	00.45
TOTAL	**£12.09**
DINNERS	**£52.76**
TOTAL WITH DINNERS	**£64.85**

Already accounted for: olives, teriyaki sauce, red lentils, mixed herbs, Worcestershire Sauce, mayo, garlic, onions, spring onions.

Notes on Breakfasts and Lunches for Summer, Week One

Cornflakes with Kiwi
Add half a kiwi alongside each bowl of cornflakes to scoop out with a teaspoon, or scatter a peeled, finely sliced half kiwi over each bowlful.

Herbed Tomatoes on Toast
Chop up 3 tomatoes very finely, then gently warm in a saucepan with one tablespoon of tomato puree, 1 teaspoon mixed herbs and some salt and pepper. Cook very gently for another minute, then pile onto warm toast.

Wheat Biscuits with Cinnamon Apples
Serve the biscuits with one apple per person, sliced and sprinkled with cinnamon.

Muffins with Celery and Peanut Butter
Chop up 2 stalks of celery finely, then mix with 3 tablespoons peanut butter and a splash of teriyaki sauce. Spread on toasted muffins.

Toast with Cinnamon Spiced Marmalade
A sprinkling of cinnamon mixed into your marmalade makes all the difference! Use of ratio of about ¼ teaspoon cinnamon to 1 teaspoon marmalade.

Pitta bread with Teriyaki Mushrooms and Cannellini Beans
Slice 200g mushrooms, drain the tin of cannellini beans and combine thoroughly with 3 tablespoons Teriyaki sauce; leave to marinate overnight. The next morning, stir-fry until the mushrooms are cooked but still quite firm. Pile into toasted pittas.

Wholemeal Wraps with Tomato, Beansprout and Garlic Rice
Cook 340g rice according to packet instructions, but 3 minutes before the end of the cooking time add 2 chopped cloves of garlic. Once you have drained the rice, cover it with foil until cooled. Chop 3 tomatoes and add them to the rice with the remaining beansprouts and some salt and pepper. Pack into 4 wraps.

Rolls with Peanut Butter and Sweetcorn
Drain half a tin of sweetcorn, chop roughly, then mix into the peanut butter before spreading.

Tacos with Rice, Kiwi and Sliced Olives (Needs to be started the night before)
Cook the rice (60g per person) the night before. Finely slice 4 olives per person and mix into the rice along with a very finely chopped onion mixed with 1 teaspoon mirin (this will remove some of the acidity from the onions) and allow to infuse overnight. In the morning, add 2 peeled, chopped kiwis and 1 heaped tablespoon of vegan mayo. Check the seasoning – it may be salty enough with the residual brine from the olives. If you're packing up the tacos, rather than keeping the wraps open, roll them up like a cigar to keep the filling in.

Pittas with Teriyaki Celery and Peanut Sweetcorn Rice (Needs to be started the night before)
As always, allow 60g rice per person. Once it is cooked, add in 2 stalks of finely chopped celery and 2 tablespoons Teriyaki Sauce. Allow to infuse overnight. Stir in one and a half tins of drained sweetcorn mixed with 2 tablespoons peanut butter in the morning, then pack into pittas.

Rolls with Red Lentil Spread
See over for the recipe for the spread

Leftover Roast with Herbed Rice Salad
This week's lentil roast is equally good served cold, sliced. Cook up 340g rice, then while it is still hot add 2 teaspoon dried mixed herbs and a finely chopped clove of garlic. Once cool, mix in two chopped stalks of celery and 4 chopped apples.

Final notes: 1. If my maths is correct, you will use 960g from the 1kg packet of rice, so there is a little room for manoeuvre. 2. The beansprouts used here are 60g reserved from this week's Chow Mien – raw goes a lot further, obviously, and it is not the main ingredient.

Red Lentil Spread

This isn't a looker (we gave up trying to make a pretty photo out of it) but looks don't always convey the magic within as we all know, and this is very tasty, so here is a picture of some lentils.

Ingredients

250g red lentils

2 onions, chopped

2 cloves garlic, chopped

1 teaspoon vegan Worcestershire Sauce

2 teaspoon mixed dried herbs

2 tablespoons vegan mayo

Salt and pepper

1 tablespoon olive oil

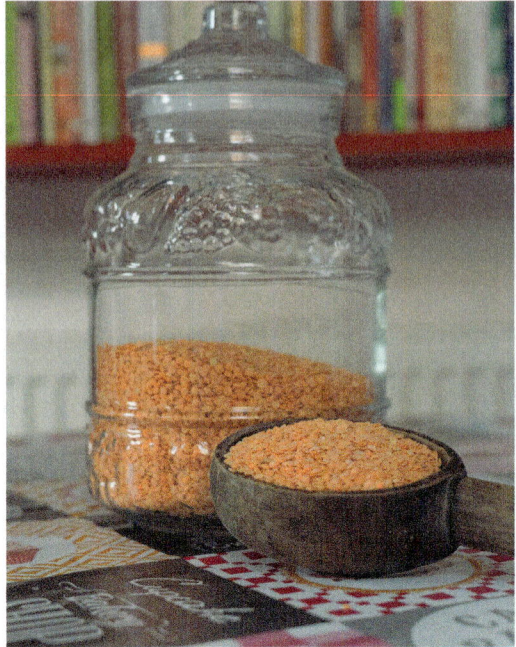

Method

1) Cover the lentils in water and leave about a 5 cm margin at the top.

2) Bring to the boil, then turn it down and simmer for about 10–15 minutes or until the water has evaporated, whichever comes first. What you are after are soft lentils, not mush. If necessary, add more boiling water from the kettle if it looks as if it will boil dry.

3) While the lentils are still warm, stir in the mixed dried herbs.

4) Lightly fry the onions until translucent, then add the garlic and fry for another minute.

5) Combine the herby lentils with the garlic, onion and Worcestershire Sauce.

6) When this mixture is cool, add the mayo. Stir well, then taste. Add salt and pepper according to your taste; do this gradually, so that you don't over salt.

Dinners for Summer, Week Two

1. Beer Battered Tempura

2. Pasta Provencal with Pistachios

3. Tomato and Walnut Pilaf

4. New Potatoes in a Malay Scented Sauce

5. Summer Flan with Almond
   and Tomato Salad

6. Buckwheat Pancakes with Sausages,
   Roasted Vegetables and Garlic Mushrooms

7. Baked Pancakes Stuffed with
   Sweet and Sour Vegetables

Shopping List for Dinners for Summer, Week Two

	Prices
spring onions	00.37
mixed chillies	00.57
2 packs of 3 mixed peppers at 92p each	01.84
200g kale	00.65
one lemon	00.29
one cauliflower	00.75
one head of broccoli	00.39
3 x 150g button mushrooms at 67p each	02.14
5 medium aubergines at 65p each	03.25
fresh ginger	00.47
one cucumber	00.49
160g mange tout	00.99
500g chestnut mushrooms	01.90
150g asparagus	00.95
500g baby carrots	00.45
one head of celery	00.53
1 kg baby potatoes	00.80
400g packet beansprouts	00.60
100g tenderstem broccoli	00.95
6 loose courgettes	01.35
1 kg onions	00.59
225g vine ripened cherry tomatoes	01.00
250g cherry tomatoes	00.58
pack 6 medium tomatoes	00.69
one garlic bulb	00.25

Fridge

1 litre plant milk	00.59
dairy free sunflower spread	00.85
200g vegan cheddar	02.00

300g silken tofu	01.25

Freezer

907g frozen sweetcorn	00.69
Pack of 6 own brand vegetarian sausages 01.50	

Cupboard

soy sauce	00.42
chopped tomatoes	00.34
1 litre carbonated water	00.17
500ml beer	00.89
1 litre sunflower oil	01.09
jar of olives in brine	00.59
550g pasta	00.45
125g packet of pistachio nuts	01.25
200g peanuts	00.48
432g can of pineapple	00.65
2 x 130g walnuts at 1.29 each	02.58
275g long grain brown rice	00.99
290g apple sauce	00.37
80g sundried tomato paste	00.75
15g jar Herbes de Provence	00.69
40g turmeric	00.49
90g jar galangal paste	01.30
400ml tin of coconut milk	00.80
75g plantain crisps	00.50
250 cornflour	00.75
1 kg buckwheat flour (Holland and Barrett)	01.99
110g garam masala	00.60
150g blanched almonds	01.65
1 kg gram flour	01.40
TOTAL	**£50.91**

Already accounted for: teriyaki sauce, tomato puree, plain flour, baking powder, caster sugar and Dijon mustard.

Beer Battered Tempura

Just like traditional tempura, this should not sit around as it quickly goes soggy, so the trick is to have the vegetables and batter prepared before you start to heat the oil. A half and half mixture of beer and water produced the best result after experimentation; it tasted far too beery without the water, but with it the flavour was more subtle. A nuance of beer sets the batter on a different trajectory without drowning it. Practically any vegetables (except potatoes) are good for tempura. There are many recipes available detailing different combinations of flours but the important thing to remember if you want to experiment is that you do need raising agents (baking powder, fizzy water) if you are using a plain flour.

Ingredients

2 red peppers, deseeded and sliced
1 medium cauliflower, broken into small florets
4 leaves of kale
Washed head of broccoli, broken into small florets
115g gram flour

115g corn flour
2 teaspoons baking powder
150ml fizzy water from the fridge
150ml beer from the fridge
1 teaspoon salt
Sunflower oil for deep-frying

Method

1) Put kitchen paper on 4 or 5 plates in readiness for the hot vegetables.

2) Sift together the dry ingredients, then make a well in the centre.

3) Pour in the beer and fizzy water, whisking as you go until everything is well combined.

4) Heat the oil in a large saucepan (about 4cm high) until bubbling but not smoking. Test a smidgeon of batter in it; if it puffs up and goes brown, it is ready.

5) Submerge a few of the vegetables in the batter and gently toss to coat, then carefully lower into the hot oil using tongs, making sure you allow plenty of room for the batter to puff up. Keep checking the oil – turn the heat off if it seems as if it is starting to smoke, turning on again when necessary.

6) Once the battered vegetables are a golden brown, remove with a strainer (the wider the better) and lay in a single layer on the prepared plate.

7) Continue in this way until you have battered all the vegetables; they only take about 3 minutes so you don't have to worry about the waiting vegetables getting cold.

8) Transfer to a pretty plate and serve with plum sauce or sweet chilli sauce.

Pasta Provencal with Pistachios

Sometimes just adding one off-piste ingredient to a classic dish ruins it, but if you're lucky it can really unlock its flavours. Pistachios are native to Iran but grow well wherever the sun shines, which includes Southern Europe, so this addition was a logical guess with lip-smacking results.

Ingredients

500g pasta
4 medium courgettes, chopped into 2cm cubes
250g button mushrooms, halved
2 onions, chopped finely
2 medium aubergines, chopped into small 1 cm cubes
1 red pepper, chopped

1 tin chopped tomatoes
2 tablespoons sundried tomato puree
2 teaspoons Herbes de Provence
1 tablespoon oil
1 small packet pistachios
1 small jar green olives, drained

Method

1) Cook the pasta according to the instructions (usually 11 minutes).

2) First fry the onion until soft, then add the rest of the veg.

3) Stir-fry for five minutes, then add the tomatoes, sun dried tomato puree and herbs, then gently simmer for 10 minutes.

4) Add the olives and nuts, then heat through just enough to warm them.

Tomato and Walnut Pilaf

Pilaf, a Middle Eastern dish (often) isn't really supposed to be cooked in the oven, but if you use brown rice, which has a firmer texture when cooked, the grains stay appetisingly separate, as they should be.

Some people find the taste of brown rice overpowers the other ingredients in the dish, but if you emphasise its nutty flavour by adding real nuts, and offset its firmness with soft tomatoes, you may well find it can be subtle too.

Ingredients

200g halved walnuts
225g vine cherry tomatoes, halved; reserve 4 x 2 tomatoes for serving
2 garlic cloves, chopped finely
2 medium onions, chopped fairly finely
3 tablespoons sun-dried tomato paste
1 teaspoon garam masala
225g brown rice
½ litre of water combined with 2 tablespoons tomato puree
1 tablespoon olive oil

Method

1) Preheat the oven to Gas Mark 4/180°C/350°F.

2) Gently heat the oil in a wok (or, if your dish is oven to table, in that).

3) Fry the onion until translucent. Add the garam masala, then fry for another two minutes.

4) Stir in the rice, sun-dried tomato paste and tomatoes and cook for five minutes, stirring all the time.

5) Pour in the water, bring it to boil, then turn the heat down and simmer for 4 minutes, stirring now and then, but gently.

6) Add the walnuts and garlic to the mixture, and toss lightly.

7) Transfer to your casserole dish (or just to the oven if you have the right dish) and cook for 45 minutes. Let it rest for 3 minutes before serving, transfer into bowls, then garnish each one with 2 vine tomatoes.

New Potatoes in a Malay Scented Sauce

When you cook this, it reminds you why the words 'fragrant' and 'aromatic' are used ad infinitum to describe South East Asian food! This sauce is a joy to smell, cook and eat and I couldn't see any reason why it shouldn't be paired with potatoes!

Ingredients

1 tablespoon olive oil

2 medium onions, chopped

2 medium courgettes, sliced vertically then horizontally into 1 cm slices

200g aubergines – baby ones are lovely here – cubed

500g new potatoes

4 baby carrots, top and tailed, then sliced

1 teaspoon turmeric

1 teaspoon galangal paste

40g fresh ginger (peeled weight), chopped finely

1 400ml tin coconut milk

Sides: 1 cucumber, sliced; 1 x 180g cassava chips; 100g packet of peanuts

Method

1) Wash the potatoes and carrots, boil for about 12 minutes.

2) In the meantime, fry the onions gently in the oil for five minutes.

3) Add the turmeric, galangal paste and fresh ginger and fry very gently for another two minutes.

4) Add the aubergines and courgettes and fry for another five minutes.

5) Add the drained cooked potatoes and carrots, then pour in the coconut milk. Stir thoroughly, then simmer for five minutes until the vegetables are tender.

6) Serve with sliced cucumber, peanuts and plantain chips for people to help themselves.

Summer Flan with Almond and Tomato Salad

(Some of the tomatoes for the salad need to be dehydrated the night before – see below.)

If you want to speed this up, you can use bought shortcrust. This will add another £1 to your shopping total. This is such a tasty flan to make and is not time consuming if you start cooking the potatoes and carrots so they are ready when the pastry case is: put the water on to boil before you start anything else. Once your pastry is rolled, check it alongside the tin you wish to use before you commit yourself – you'll obviously need about 2 cm margin for the sides.

Ingredients

For the Flan
3 cloves garlic, finely chopped
1 onion, very finely chopped
1 teaspoon Dijon mustard
100g vegan mature cheddar (half a 200g packet)
300g silken tofu
17 baby carrots, cooked

6 florets of tender new broccoli
10 small potatoes, cooked
10 asparagus tips

For the Almond and Tomato Salad
100g blanched almonds
150g cherry tomatoes
4 medium tomatoes

Method

1) The night before, slice 4 medium tomatoes vertically, then put them on a lined baking tray on the lowest setting of the oven overnight.

2) In the morning, allow them to cool, then put them in an airtight container until you make the salad.

3) To make the shortcrust, rub the margarine into the flour until it resembles breadcrumbs. Add the salt, then add 6 tablespoons of very cold water, preferably putting ice cubes in a bowl, then adding the water to it. Using a palette knife, gradually incorporate the water into the mixture by taking the knife around the sides and down the middle, until you have a soft ball of dough.

4) With the flat of your hands, pat the dough on the side of the ball to create four straight sides, then roll out enough to line a square tin. (Obviously revise this if you don't have one; if you are rolling a circle, push the rolling pin in one direction, from the middle to the perimeter, as if you are following the spokes of a wheel).

5) Line your flan case and trim the edges. Bake blind for ten minutes at 200°C/400°F/Gas Mark 6.

6) Water fry the onions until translucent.

7) Add the garlic and fry for a further 2 minutes.

8) Blend together the tofu, mustard and cheese in the food processor, then add the onions and garlic.

9) Remove the case from the oven, pile in the tofu mixture, then arrange the vegetables as you like them; if the tin is square, it looks effective if you arrange alternating vegetables pointing towards the centre, as shown. But of course the artistry is up to you! Bake for 15–20 minutes, until the filling is firm and the carrots and green vegetables have a 'grilled' look.

10) For the salad, mix 100g blanched almonds with 150g cherry tomatoes and the 4 medium tomatoes you dehydrated overnight.

Buckwheat Pancakes with Sausages, Roasted Vegetables and Garlic Mushrooms

The nutty flavour of buckwheat pancakes is one of the loveliest, most palatable way of incorporating grains into your diet.

Ingredients

Buckwheat Pancakes
290ml plant milk
2 tablespoons apple sauce
A pinch salt
1 teaspoon sunflower oil
115g buckwheat flour
1 teaspoon Herbes de Provence
1 teaspoon vegetable oil, for cooking

Garlic Mushrooms
500g chestnut mushrooms, washed and sliced

3 cloves garlic
30g vegan margarine

Roasted Veg
100g cherry tomatoes
1 small aubergine
1 orange pepper
1 yellow pepper
2 tablespoons olive oil
4 vegan sausages, sliced into discs

Method

1) First make the roasted vegetables: preheat the oven to Gas Mark 8/230°C/425°F. Cut one slice of orange pepper and one slice of yellow pepper for your garnish, then cut the rest of the peppers and the aubergine into 1 cm squares. Halve the tomatoes. Toss with oil

and salt and roast for 10–15 minutes, tossing and turning again after about 7 minutes. Remove from the oven, turn the oven down to Gas Mark 3/170°C/325°F, and open the oven door to cool the oven down a little (it will burn the pancakes otherwise). Transfer to a saucepan.

2) You can now use two rings on the hob to prepare the sausages and mushrooms, which you can then put on the two back burners, turned off, when you make the pancakes, and reheat them just before assembling the stuffed pancakes: melt the margarine, add the garlic and mushrooms, and fry until they are tender but still firm; on the other ring, fry the sausage slices in a little oil until they are just slightly under browned. Turn both hobs off, then put the pans on the back burners.

3) Make the pancakes: put the plant milk, apple sauce, salt and oil into a large bowl and mix well. Sift the buckwheat flour into another bowl. Stir in the herbs. Add the flour and herbs to the milk mixture gradually, stirring constantly until a smooth batter is formed. Allow the batter to rest for thirty minutes prior to cooking.

4) To make a stack of eight pancakes, you need to have a plate with ten sheets of greaseproof paper cut roughly to the size of the plate all ready; you begin and end with a sheet of paper, and interweave each pancake with a sheet. Add a teaspoon of oil to a hot pan, pour in an eighth of the mixture and cook for 1–2 minutes on each side, or until lightly browned on each side. Remove from the pan and place on the plate lined with its first sheet of greaseproof paper. As you cook each subsequent pancake, keep them all warm by covering the plate in a tent of foil, removing and replacing as you add each sheet and pancake) and putting in the preheated oven.

5) Now for the assembly. Turn the heat on under the sausages, mushrooms and roasted vegetables, adding an extra 1 teaspoon oil to the vegetables. Gently finish browning the sausages and reheating the mushrooms and vegetables, stirring now and then to prevent sticking, while you get the pancakes out of the oven.

6) Begin with a pancake, cover with the sausages, top with a pancake, add a layer of roasted vegetables, another pancake, garlic mushrooms, and then the final pancake. Garnish with one slice of orange pepper and one slice of yellow pepper and put sausage slices around the edge.

NB: You will be left with four pancakes. If you don't want them for tomorrow's dinner, they freeze excellently; just make sure they are well wrapped in foil, and keep the interweaving layers of greaseproof paper. Otherwise put in the fridge for tomorrow.

Baked Pancakes Stuffed with Sweet and Sour Vegetables

The joy of buckwheat pancakes (originally from Brittany) is that they can be partnered with almost any cuisine from anywhere on the globe because their flavour is so nuttily subtle. You could pair them with a spicy dahl, or a creamy béchamel sauce with vegetables, or Tex Mex ingredients, or a satay; they are truly the culinary equivalent of the blank canvas. Now, Brittany meets Beijing (sort of) with pancakes and a mouth-watering sweet and sour sauce.

Ingredients

Pancakes

If you are not using the pancakes left from yesterday, halve the number of ingredients listed for them, except the oil and herbs, then follow the recipe given.

Sweet and Sour Vegetables
100g button mushrooms
1 packet fresh beansprouts
2 200g mange tout
30g vegan margarine
1425g tin pineapple
1 red chilli, chopped
2 spring onions, thinly sliced
1 teaspoon cornflour
The zest and juice of one lemon
2 teaspoons sugar

Method

1) If you haven't refrigerated some pancakes from yesterday, make four according to the instructions, only with half the ingredients, as mentioned above (except for the oil and herbs). Preheat the oven to Gas Mark 5/190°C/375°F.

2) In one pan, stir-fry the mangetout and celery together for four minutes. Add the button mushrooms, fry for another 3 minutes, then turn off the pan until you are ready to add the following sauce:

   a. Melt the margarine in a wok and sauté the onion over a low heat until translucent. Add the chopped chilli, combine with the onion and stir-fry for two minutes.

   b. Add the pineapple (with its juice) and spring onions, stir well, then gently simmer for 5 minutes.

   c. Mix the lemon juice, sugar and cornflower together to make a smooth paste, then add this paste and the lemon zest to the pan.

   d. Tip this sauce onto the vegetables, stir well, then heat gently for two minutes.

5) Grease a lasagne or oval dish. Lay each pancake out flat and put two tablespoons of sweet and sour vegetable into the middle of each one. Bring the two sides together so that they overlap, then carefully line them up side by side in the dish; one can go along the top if you run out of room. Take the rest of the filling and spread it over the pancakes.

6) Bake for 10 minutes on Number 5, just long enough to slightly brown the vegetables.

Suggestions and Shopping List for Breakfasts and Lunches for Summer, Week Two

BREAKFASTS

Porridge with Sultanas and Vanilla

Muffins with Marmalade and Crushed Walnuts

Toast with Teriyaki Tomatoes and Spring Onions

Cornflakes with Crunchy Apples

Overnight Oats with Mandarin Oranges and
Vanilla (preserve juice from can)

Cornflakes with Mandarin Scented Sultanas
(use juice from Mandarin oranges)

Spicy Sausage and Beans on Toast

LUNCHES

Pittas with Turmeric Rice, Tenderstem Broccoli and Peas

Wraps with Quick Pickled Red Cabbage and Green Lentil Salad

Rolls with Green Lentil Spread and Sweetcorn

Buckwheat Pancakes with Baked Beans and Crispy Onions

Pittas with Teriyaki Giant Couscous, Red Cabbage Coleslaw, Green Beans

Buckwheat Pancakes with Baked Beans and Crispy Onion

Tacos with Curried Mixed Lentils (including
sultanas, celery and red cabbage)

Shopping List

4 muffins	00.39
4 x 410g baked beans at 23p each	00.92
2 x 6 pitta bread at 42p each	00.84
1 kg porridge oats	00.75
312 tin mandarin oranges	00.44
500g sultanas	00.88
6 tomatoes	00.59
1 kg green beans	00.85
1 red cabbage	00.55
4 large brown rolls	00.45
8 brown wraps	00.75
900g frozen peas	00.76
800g loaf brown bread	00.50
500g own brand cornflakes	00.38
6 own brand vegan sausages	01.50
500g green lentils	00.75
454g marmalade	00.27
TOTAL	**£11.57**
DINNERS	**£50.91**
TOTAL WITH DINNERS	**£62.48**

Already accounted for: Teriyaki sauce, chillies, vanilla extract, white wine vinegar, Worcestershire Sauce, rice, green beans, celery, tender stream broccoli, turmeric, garam masala, sweetcorn giant couscous, onions, red lentils, spring onions, vegan mayo, walnuts (70g) and ingredients for buckwheat pancakes.

Notes on Breakfasts and Lunches for Summer, Week Two

Porridge with Sultanas and Vanilla (start the night before)
Put 2 tablespoons of sultanas in a bowl and cover with water. Add 1 teaspoon of vanilla extract. Stir and soak overnight. In the morning, drain well and stir into your porridge.

Muffins with Marmalade and Crushed Walnuts
Crush the nuts left over from the pilaf (there will be about 60g) and scatter over the marmalade on toasted muffins.

Toast with Teriyaki Tomatoes and Spring Onions (start the night before)
Chop up two top and tailed spring onions, discarding any tough leaves. Chop up for tomatoes, mix with the onion, then add 2 tablespoons teriyaki sauce. Leave to infuse overnight, then lightly fry in the morning until the onions are translucent. Pile onto toast.

Cornflakes with Crunchy Apples (start the night before)
Leave the apples (one each) in the fridge overnight and they will be crunchier. Chop up in the morning and add to the cornflake bowls.

Mandarin and Vanilla Overnight Oats (start the night before, obviously)
Add 1 teaspoon vanilla extra and a tin of mandarin oranges to the oats when you are soaking them. Reserve the juice for the next breakfast.

Cornflakes with Mandarin Vanilla Scented Sultanas
Soak 2 tablespoons sultanas in the juice from yesterday's can of mandarin oranges. Add 1 teaspoon vanilla. In the morning, drain thoroughly and divide between the bowls of cornflakes.

Spicy Sausage and Beans on Toast
Allow the veggie sausages to defrost slightly, then slice them into coins. Grill until brown, then put them in a saucepan with two tins of baked beans and a pinch of garam masala. Heat until the beans are simmering, then pile onto toast.

Pittas with Turmeric Rice, Tenderstem Broccoli and Peas
Add 1 teaspoon turmeric to the rice as you are boiling it. Defrost 4 tablespoons peas and add it to the rice (bring it back to the boil) 3 minutes before the end of the cooking time. Drain the rice, transferring

the hot water into another saucepan. In this water, gently simmer the broccoli for about 5 minutes, drain, chop, then mix with the rice and peas. Add salt to taste, then stuff toasted pittas.

Wraps with Quick Pickled Red Cabbage and Green Lentil Salad

Thoroughly chop about an eighth of a red cabbage and tenderise for a while in 2 tablespoons white wine vinegar while you make the salad: boil 150g green lentils for about 20–30 minutes, erring on the side of al dente. When the lentils are drained but still warm, add a thumbnail size peeled and chopped knob of ginger, 4 chopped baby carrots, and half a very finely chopped onion. Add salt to taste, mix with the drained red cabbage, then stuff your wraps.

Rolls with Green Lentil Spread and Sweetcorn

Follow the recipe for Red Lentil Spread, (using 250g green lentils) but obviously the green lentils take longer to cook than the red (about 10 minutes longer). Stir in 2 tablespoons thawed sweetcorn, then fill the rolls.

Buckwheat Pancakes with Baked Beans and Crispy Onions

See the recipe for Buckwheat Pancakes earlier. Make 8 and reserve 4 for the day after tomorrow. (Interweave with baking parchment, cover, and keep in the fridge until needed). Fry two chopped onions until crispy. Heat 2 tins of beans, spread over the pancakes, and top with crispy onions.

Pittas with Teriyaki Giant Couscous, Red Cabbage Coleslaw and Green Beans

Steam 500g green beans for about 15 minutes. Chop up another eighth of a red cabbage and mix it with enough vegan mayo to coat. To cook the giant couscous, cover it with water then add a margin of about 5cm. Simmer for about 10 minutes. Stir the teriyaki sauce into the cooked couscous. Mix everything gently and stuff the pittas.

Buckwheat Pancakes with Garlic Green Beans and Baked Herby Onions

Preheat the oven to 180°C/350°F/Gas Mark 4 and during this time remove the pancakes from the refrigerator and allow to come to room temperature. Thoroughly chop two onions very finely and mix with 2 teaspoons dried herbs. Spread the pancakes with the herby onion mixture, roll up, then wrap tightly in foil. Bake for 15 minutes – you want the onion to soften, but you don't want the already cooked pancakes to blacken, so make sure there are no gaps in the foil. During this time, steam 500g green beans for about 15 minutes. About 5 minutes before the end of the steaming time, sprinkle on the two finely chopped cloves of garlic. With luck, the pancakes and beans should be ready at the same time. (If not, turn off the oven and keep the pancakes warm in the residual heat, or just keep the lid on the steamer, whichever one is lagging behind).

Tacos with Curried Mixed Lentils (start the night before)

Cook 150g green lentils with 1 teaspoon each of turmeric and garam masala. Once drained, keep in the saucepan with the lid to allow the steam to help the spices infuse further. Stir in 2 tablespoons sultanas, 2 chopped stalks of celery, an eighth of a red cabbage, chopped, and 2 tablespoons vegan mayo. Allow the lentils to absorb the flavours overnight before filling your tacos in the morning.

Dinners for Summer, Week Three

1. Sausages with Russian Salad

2. Pasta in a Miso and Mushroom Broth

3. Dip in the Week

4. Tri-Tomato Swedish Meatballs
   with Udon Noodles

5. Easy Cheesy Beany Stew with Spinach

6. Pepper and Chickpea Cutlets
   with Sweet and Sour Sauce

7. Meze with a Light Japanese Touch

Shopping List for Dinners for Summer, Week Three

Vegetables/Fruit

750g organic onions	00.95
750g organic carrots	00.95
packet of 3 garlic bulbs	00.85
1.5kg organic potatoes	01.15
mixed chillies	00.57
pack of three mixed peppers	00.92
one head of celery	00.53
500g chestnut mushrooms	01.90
2 x 350g cherry tomatoes at 71p each	01.42
200g baby spinach	01.39
2 lemons at 29p each	00.58
1 cucumber	00.49
25g fresh chives	00.60
200g radishes	00.48

Fridge

300g silken tofu	01.25
200g vegan cheese	02.00
1 litre plant milk	01.40
8 vegan sausages	02.49
250g vegan margarine	00.85

Cupboard

tomato puree	00.37
chopped tomatoes x 2 at 34p each	00.68
1.5kg plain flour	00.45
500g tricolour pasta	01.00
800g wholemeal bread	01.00
560g tomato ketchup	00.55
2 x 6 wholemeal pittas at 42p each	00.84
500g light brown sugar	00.69
272g tinned pineapple	00.57
4 x 400g tinned chickpeas at 33p each	01.32

500g vegan mayo (e.g. Chippa)	01.00
95g miso paste	02.00
90g harissa paste	01.10
435g tin of refried beans	01.36
190g pickled garlic	00.85
150g blue tortilla chips	01.69
95g mini breadsticks	00.95
50g jar jerk seasoning	01.00
100g tube sun-dried tomato paste	00.75
4 x 410g baked beans	02.00
300g jar ginger paste	01.20
43g wasabi paste	01.41
500g yellow split peas	00.55
200g sea salt	00.55
40g dried onion	00.65
60g pickled garlic	00.59
300g udon noodles	01.30

Freezer

500g vegan mince	01.40
TOTAL	**47.69**

Already accounted for: cornflour, olive oil, apple sauce, soy sauce, vegan Worcestershire sauce and teriyaki sauce.

Sausages with Russian Salad

People familiar with Russian salads will know that Russians sometimes cook their salad vegetables, then allow them to cool, rather than eating them raw. For this reason these salads naturally compliment American style potato salads, which need to be cooked by their very nature. Cooked vegetables allowed to cool may suggest an unappealing stolid blandness, but if you serve best quality vegetables at room temperature, and allow them to absorb a well-seasoned mayonnaise in advance, they are flavourful and satisfying as well as inexpensive.

Ingredients

4 large organic carrots, diced
700g organic potatoes, diced
4 sticks celery, sliced
2 heaped tablespoons vegan mayo

1 teaspoon pepper
1 teaspoon sea salt
8 sausages

Method

1) Depending on the size of the dice, boil the carrots and potatoes (separately) for 8–10 minutes until they are tender.

2) Season the mayonnaise with the salt and pepper and set aside.

3) Drain the vegetables and toss them, while still warm, in the seasoned mayonnaise. This helps the absorption of the flavour.

4) Slice the celery and add to the mix.

5) Leave for a least an hour and serve at room temperature. About ten minutes before you want to serve up, grill or fry the sausages.

Pasta in a Miso and Mushroom Broth

Udon noodles in Japan, which are made from unleavened wheat dough, like pasta, are often served in a miso broth. This got me thinking that miso would make a good pasta sauce, taste-wise, but it does texture-wise too because, when slightly thickened, it coats the pasta wonderfully; it is especially effective with 'curly' pasta. Coloured pasta is better here because you need to add a splash of colour to enliven the monochrome of the beige-like brown.

Ingredients

12oz pasta
500ml water
1 tablespoon cornflour
1 tablespoon soy sauce
1 tablespoon miso
2 cloves garlic
1 tablespoon sunflower oil (olive is too strong and competes with the taste of the miso)
500g chestnut mushrooms
Black pepper

Method

1) Get the pasta underway (packets usually specify boiling for 11 minutes) while you get on with the sauce.

2) Gently fry the garlic in the oil for one minute only.

3) Add the cornflour, and cook, stirring, for five minutes.

4) Turn off the heat and gradually add the water, stirring all the time.

5) Add the mushrooms and soy sauce, gently lift and roll to mix, and simmer until the mushrooms are tender.

6) Add the miso and cook very gently until it is absorbed in the sauce. Do not boil at any time because it destroys the beneficial nutrients in the miso.

7) Serve with the pasta.

Dip in the Week

Finding Tuesday morning a bit of a hill to climb, and Wednesday night feeling like you're well on the way to the weekend, seems to be an international phenomenon. The Americans and British call Wednesday 'hump day' and the Finnish people have dubbed it 'little Saturday', and often party on that night. Here is a relaxed, miniaturised way to celebrate this special day with some typical party food in the form of spectacularly easy dips. Add some carrot batons and green pepper strips for scooping alongside the breadsticks and tortilla chips, and you have your five-a-day as well as a laid back, fun mini Saturday night.

Ingredients

1 packet blue tortilla chips
1 packet mini breadsticks

Moroccan Refried Beans
One 400g tin of refried beans
1 teaspoon harissa paste

Tomato and Two-Garlic Salsa
500g tomatoes
Cloves garlic, chopped
2 teaspoon pickled garlic

Split Pea and Three-Onion Dip
115g split peas, cooked and cooled
30g chives, snipped with scissors into 1 cm pieces
1 teaspoon dried onion
½ teaspoon powdered garlic
½ teaspoon sea salt
1 tablespoon olive oil

Tofu Sour Cream Dip
1 300g pack of silken tofu, drained
Juice of half a lemon
Pinch of sea salt
½ – 1 teaspoon powdered garlic

Methods

1) For the Moroccan Refried Beans, stir the harissa into the refried beans and set aside.

2) For the Tomato and Two Garlic Salsa, fry the tomatoes in garlic for the salsa; allow to cool then mix in the pickled garlic.

3) For the Tofu Sour Cream Dip, blend together the silken tofu, lemon juice, sea salt and powdered garlic (to taste).

4) For the Split Pea and Three Onion Dip, process the split peas with dried onion, garlic, salt and olive oil, then stir in the chives.

5) Lay out the dips in bowls on a special dip dish if you have one, then put the tortilla chips and breadsticks in bowls or surrounding the dip, depending on the crockery you have available. If you don't have a special dip dish, putting a bowl in the middle of a plate is a good improvisation, which I am sure has occurred to you already!

Tri-Tomato Swedish Meatballs with Udon Noodles

Much loved Spaghetti and Meatballs are American/Italian in origin. This recipe gives the famous dish another two fusion twists and a big tomato hit.

*For the Swedish Meatballs

500g packet veggie mince
1 tablespoon apple sauce
1 small onion, finely chopped or grated
85g fresh white breadcrumbs

1 tablespoon sun-dried tomato puree
1 tablespoon tomato ketchup
1 tablespoon freshly chopped dill
1–2 tablespoons olive oil
1 teaspoon garlic salt

For the Garlic and Tomato Sauce

2 tins chopped tomatoes
4 cloves garlic, chopped
1 onion, chopped

1 tablespoon sun-dried tomato puree
1 tablespoon olive oil

Udon Noodles

1 x 250g dried packet Udon noodles

Method

1) Combine the mince, apple sauce, onion, breadcrumbs, sun-dried tomato puree and dill. Mix with the wooden spoon until you have a malleable mixture. If it looks too dry, add a little water, a drop at a time. If it looks too wet (it depends on the density of your breadcrumbs), add a few more breadcrumbs. Line 1–2 plates with kitchen paper.

2) Shape the mixture into slightly oversized walnuts, then heat the oil in a wide frying pan and fry in batches, adding more oil if necessary and turning for even browning, until the meatballs are brown all over. As they are cooked, lift them out with a slotted spoon and lay them on the kitchen paper to drain.

3) Next make the tomato sauce (the same pan is fine). Fry the onion in the oil until translucent, then add the remaining ingredients. Simmer for about five minutes until the garlic is tender. Now would be a good time to put on a covered pan of water for the noodles.

4) Add the meatballs to the sauce and spoon it over (you don't need as much room for the meatballs this time as you won't be frisking them around the pan).

5) Reheat the meatballs in the simmering sauce for about five minutes, remembering also to add the noodles to the other pan when the water comes to boil.

6) Keep the meatballs and sauce on a very low light if they are ready before the noodles.

7) Serve the meatballs and sauce on a bed of freshly cooked noodles.

*If time is pressing, obviously you can buy ready-made (ASDA have 400g meatless meatballs for £1.50 at time of writing) and follow the instructions; if you would still like the tomato shot, add the puree and ketchup to the sauce instead.

Easy Cheesy Beany Stew with Spinach

A loveable, scoopable and affordable blend of iron and protein-rich foods in a light summer stew. If it comes across as a manic (con)fusion of beans on middle eastern toast with an anglicised Sag Paneer, please still give it a try; the flavours and textures make this so much more appealing than it may sound.

Ingredients

2 tins baked beans
200g vegan cheddar; grate 150g and reserve 50g for garnish
1 packet of fresh spinach

4 medium tomatoes, chopped
2 cloves of garlic
To serve: 6 pitta breads

Method

1) Fry the garlic until soft on a fairly low light.

2) Add the chopped tomatoes and fry for two minutes.

3) Add the beans and cheddar and stir gently until the cheese has blended in.

4) Finally, add the spinach plus a few cubes of the vegan cheese as garnish.

5) Pop the pitta bread under the grill or in the toaster just before you serve up. Cut each pitta in half horizontally for scooping purposes.

Pepper and Chickpea Cutlets with Sweet and Sour Sauce

This classic Chinese sauce often graces food from other parts of the world and there are an infinitesimal number of recipes for it out there – we've all made it our own! It certainly elevates these appetising but humble cutlets by combining the earthy with the unexpected to maximise both budget and flavour. This uses a bag of 3 assorted peppers.

Sweet and Sour Sauce

Make this first, then you can simply reheat it when the cutlets are ready.

Ingredients

1 onion, chopped finely

1 red or orange pepper, chopped roughly

1 425g can of pineapple in juice; you need the juice and the fruit (chopped if you can't find pineapple pieces)

1 green chilli

One 3 cm square of ginger root, chopped finely

2 tablespoons soy sauce

2 heaped teaspoons brown sugar

2 tablespoons tomato puree

Juice of one lemon (but zest it first for the cutlets)

Method

1) Water fry the onion until translucent, then add the pepper, chilli, garlic and ginger and fry for another two minutes.

2) Add the soy sauce, chopped tinned pineapple with its juice, lemon juice, brown sugar and tomato paste. Mix thoroughly.

3) Blend all the ingredients together by pulsing the food processor until you have a thick sauce with some pieces intact.

Pepper and Chickpea Cutlets

Ingredients

1 x 240g can chickpeas (drained weight)
1 onion, finely chopped
1 green pepper, chopped
1 red pepper, chopped
2 cloves of garlic, chopped very finely
30g vegan margarine

2 large cooked potatoes
2 tablespoons soy sauce
Zest of a lemon
Grinding of black pepper
Flour to coat, if wished
Small amount of oil for frying

Method

1) Mash the chickpeas together with the margarine and potatoes. Grind in some pepper to taste.

2) Beat in the onion, peppers, garlic, soy sauce and zest of a lemon. Allow to cool.

3) With lightly floured hands, shape the mixture into rough cutlet shapes. Put two aside for tomorrow and shape again into little balls.*

4) Lightly fry in oil (use a non-stick pan if possible) until golden brown on both sides.

*If following this week's menus

Meze with a Japanese Twist

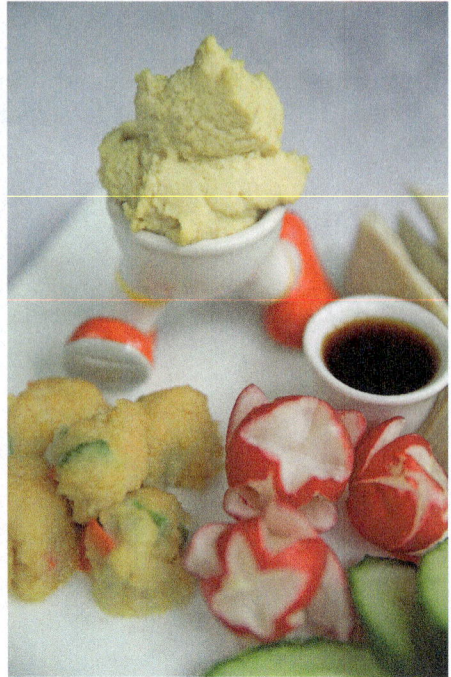

Wasabi gives hummus a wonderful kick and, for some reason I can't fathom, makes it last longer. The teriyaki sauce here is simply a bottled one, because it is a versatile condiment to have in your store cupboard and lasts a very long time. The little miniaturised chickpea cutlets have been saved from yesterday; if you didn't cook them, you could factor in about £2 for ready-made falafel, for example, or between £1–£1.50, for some falafel mix at your chosen supermarket, if you haven't the time to make the little cutlets from scratch. This dish pleases the eye as well as the palate.

Ingredients

1 packet of pitta breads (they usually contain 6)
½ cucumber (only buy a half unless you are sure you will use the rest)
4 tablespoons Teriyaki sauce
1 small packet radishes
2 tins chickpeas, drained
1 teaspoon wasabi paste

3 tablespoons olive oil
3 tablespoons water
1 lemon
2 garlic cloves, finely chopped
½ teaspoon sea salt
1 teaspoon black pepper
12 miniature chickpea cutlets, saved from yesterday, or falafel (see above)

Method

1) First make the hummus by processing the wasabi paste, chickpeas, olive oil, garlic, the juice plus zest of a lemon, salt and pepper until you have a fairly thick puree. If you want it thinner, you could always add a little water and process again.

2) Prepare the radishes: on each radish, cut a star-shaped criss-cross type pattern at the top of the radish. Under each point, cut down two diagonal lines, like the two sides of a triangle. Using your knife at the point of each incomplete triangle, gently pull the skin away from the radish to form a petal. (There are some much more complicated radish roses on YouTube if you are feeling fancy pants).

3) Put the teriyaki sauce into little pots, one per person.

4) Toast the pitta bread and cut it into broad strips.

5) Cut the cucumber into slices, on the slant.

6) On each plate put a little pot of wasabi hummus, another of teriyaki sauce, some pitta strips (6 pittas divided between you), three cucumber slices, 3 radish roses and 5 miniature chickpea cutlets.

Suggestions and Shopping List for Breakfasts and Lunches for Summer, Week Three

BREAKFASTS

Fruit Salad Porridge

Bran flakes with Sultanas

Muffins with Garlic Mushrooms

Bran flakes with Plums

Jerky Beans on Toast

Overnight Oats with Plum and Vanilla

Toasted Peanut Butter and Mango Chutney Sandwiches

LUNCHES

Pittas with Harissa Hummus, Red Cabbage and Round Lettuce

Wraps with Cheese, Tomatoes and Coral Coleslaw

Rolls with Coronation Nutty Split Peas (mayo, sultanas etc.)

Cheese and Mango Chutney Sandwiches

Jerk Sausage, Marmalade Relish and Cannelli Bean Burritos

Cheese and Wasabi Cucumber Rolls

Chapattis with Tomato and Split Pea Dahl

Shopping List

200g hummus	00.59
4 muffins	00.39
2 x 410g baked beans at 23p each	00.46
2 x 6 pitta bread at 42p each	00.84
2 x 4 large brown rolls at 45p each	00.90
8 brown wraps	00.75
400g cannellini beans	00.33
750g bran flakes	00.83
200g button mushrooms	00.75
350g chapattis	00.75
2 x 500g tomatoes at 53p each	01.06
6 vegan sausages	02.00
200g vegan cheese	02.28
Half a cucumber	00.30
8 plums (400g)	00.69
440g pickled beetroot	00.52
800g wholemeal bread	00.50
70g mango chutney	00.40
340g peanut butter	00.65
1 round lettuce	00.40
TOTAL	**£15.39**
DINNERS	**£47.69**
TOTAL WITH DINNERS	**£63.08**

Already accounted for: sultanas, mayo, marmalade, red cabbage, jerk seasoning, oats, extra bread, chillies, wasabi, mustard, garlic, garam masala, split peas, carrots, Harissa and pickled garlic (latter two left over from 'Dip in the Week') .

Notes on Breakfasts and Lunches for Summer, Week Three

Fruit Salad Porridge
To each of the four porridge bowls, add 1 plum, stoned and chopped, 1 teaspoon of marmalade and 2 teaspoons sultanas. Swirl with the tip of a spoon.

Bran flakes with Sultanas
A sprinkling of sultanas on a bowl of bran makes it far more palatable and tasty, in my opinion!

Muffins with Garlic Mushrooms
As the mushrooms are toasting, lightly fry the washed, halved button mushrooms with 2 cloves of garlic, chopped finely, until the mushrooms are slightly al dente. Spread the muffins with some vegan spread and tumble on the mushrooms.

Jerky Beans on Toast
I usually allow half a tin per person, which would make 2 tins. To this I would add 1 teaspoon Jerk seasoning, but you may wish to use more or less spice, or more or fewer beans.

Overnight Oats with Plum and Vanilla (begin overnight)
Before you soak the oats overnight, add one chopped plum and a few drops of vanilla essence to each bowl. Stir well before refrigerating.

Toasted Peanut Butter and Mango Chutney Sandwiches
I prefer to mix the chutney with the peanut butter, but you may want to spread it on top – it depends on your taste. This little 70g tub will serve four because you don't need much to get the spike of preserved mango.

Pittas with Harissa Hummus, Red Cabbage and Round Lettuce
Chop up about an eighth of a red cabbage. Thoroughly mix 1 teaspoon Harissa into your hummus. Fill your pittas with some chopped, washed leaves of round lettuce, cabbage and Harissa hummus.

Wraps with Cheese, Tomatoes and Coral Coleslaw
For the recipe for Coral Coleslaw, please see over. Pair with some grated vegan cheese (save half until later), 300g halved cherry tomatoes and wrap tenderly.

Rolls with Coronation Split Peas (needs to be started the night before)

Cook 135g split peas until soft but firm (roughly 35 minutes). Once cooled, mix with 2 tablespoons peanut butter, 1 teaspoon garam masala and 1 tablespoons vegan mayo. Spread onto your rolls.

Jerk Sausage, Marmalade Relish and Cannelli Bean Burritos

Make a marmalade relish by adding a half a finely chopped onion and a pinch of garam masala to 4 tablespoons of marmalade. Mix thoroughly. Cut the sausages into coins and fry lightly with a sprinkling of jerk seasoning. Drain your beans, then divide the 3 fillings between 4 wraps. Roll up tightly, like a burrito (see Introduction to Breakfasts and Lunches). Of course, if this is all too spicy for you, marmalade and sausages are very good together – try it if you haven't before!

Cheese and Wasabi Cucumber Rolls

Finely dice half a cucumber, then put it into a bowl with ½ – 1 teaspoon wasabi. Mix gently and taste (you can always add more, but exercise caution for now)! Fold in some grated vegan cheese, then fill your rolls.

Chapatis with Tomato and Split Pea Dahl (reserved for a home lunch)

To make the split pea dahl, cook 250g split peas for 30–40 minutes until soft. Add 2 teaspoons vegan margarine, 2 cloves of garlic, one finely chopped onion, 1 teaspoon garam masala. Gently heat and stir until the marg is melted, the garlic and onion are softened and everything is incorporated. Add 700g of halved cherry tomatoes and cook until the tomatoes are very soft. Scoop up with your chapatis.

Coral Coleslaw

Another well-dressed salad which does its partner proud in the taste stakes.

Ingredients

3 medium carrots, grated (a food processor makes short work of this)*

200g red cabbage, washed and chopped,

2 pickled baby beets, pureed in the food processor

2 tablespoons vegan mayonnaise

*You don't have to worry about washing out the food processor bowl between grating the carrots and processing the beetroot as they will be combined anyway; you just obviously need to switch the grating disc for the double-bladed knife attachment.

Method

1) Mix the mayonnaise and beetroot together until you have a hot pink colour.

2) Combine it with the grated carrot and toss gently until the pink turns to coral.

3) Add the cabbage and stir to produce a coleslaw with undercover beetroot that no beetroot hater has spotted at the time of writing.

Autumn Recipes

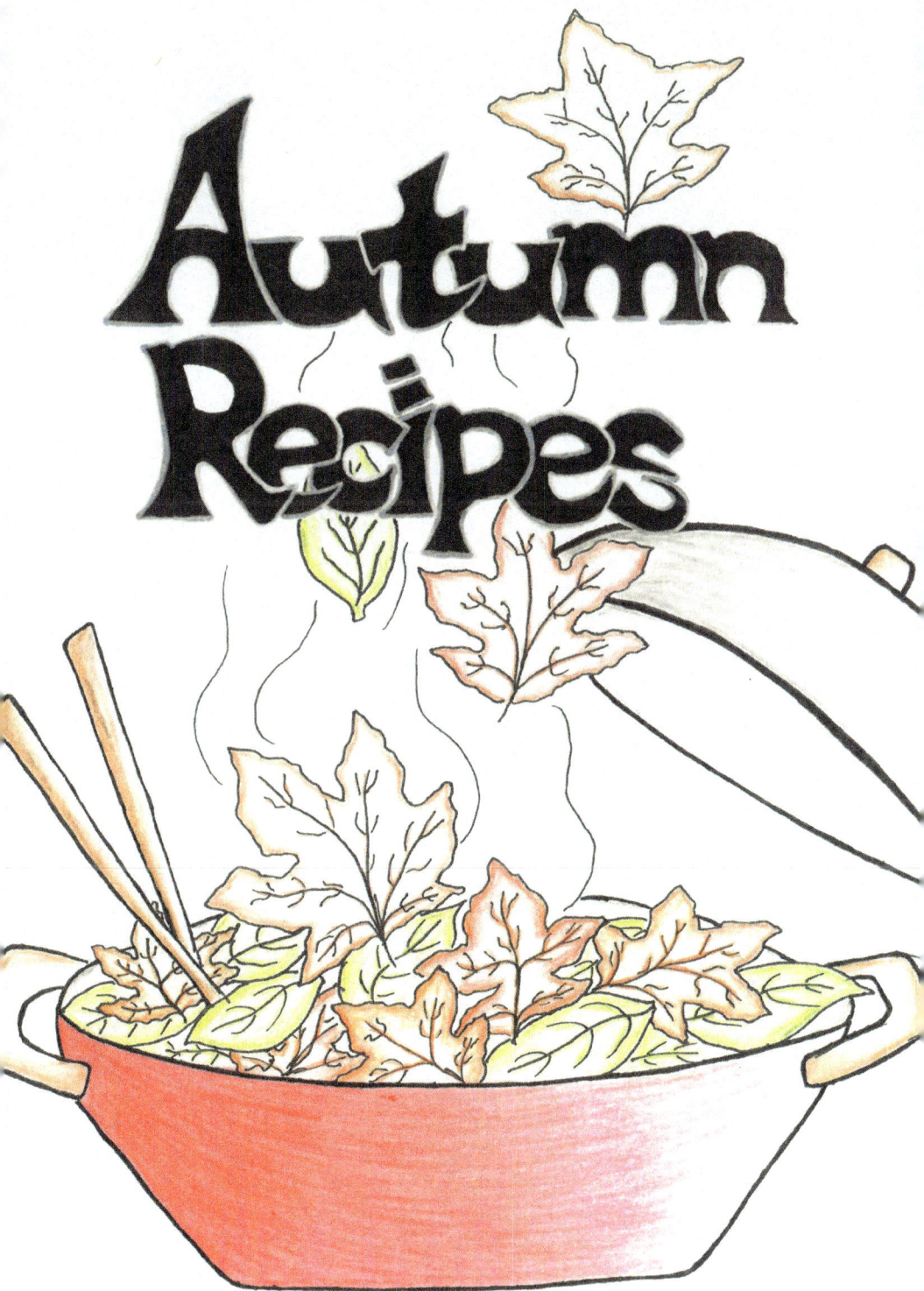

Dinners for Autumn, Week One

1. Tight Budget Tian

2. Treasure in the Tide

3. Spaghetti Plus Three Sauces

4. Ful Masala Style Broad Beans

5. Ful Masala Over Rosemary Infused Mash

6. Autumn Pie: Two Potato Bobotie

7. Lemony Pitta Hazelnut Loaf
   with Miso and Tahini Sauce

Shopping List for Dinners for Autumn, Week One

	Prices
Vegetables/Fruit	
750g organic onions	00.95
packet of 3 garlic bulbs	00.85
2 x 1.5kg organic potatoes at 1.15 each	02.30
one large aubergine	00.65
135g baby corn	00.95
2 x 200g button mushrooms at 85p each	01.70
one bunch of spring onions	00.37
Pack of 4 unwaxed lemons	00.75
7 Granny Smith apples	01.35
300g cooked baby beetroots	00.62
180g baby spinach	01.10
20g fresh rosemary	00.60
150g mixed mushrooms (shiitake, etc.)	01.50
1kg sweet potatoes	00.95
25g fresh coriander	00.95
Bag 4 x 250g cherry tomatoes at 58p each	02.32
Bag of mixed chillis	00.45
Fridge	
1 litre unsweetened soya milk	00.59
200g vegan cheddar cheese	02.00
500g vegan yoghurt	01.50
250ml soya/oat cream	01.00
200g vegan feta cheese	02.25
70g little pot of mango chutney	00.40
250g vegan marg	00.85
Cupboard	
soy sauce	00.42
tomato puree	00.37
1.5kg plain flour	00.45
170g baking powder	00.69

250g vegetable oil	00.79
500g spaghetti	00.20
2 x 6 wholemeal pitta at 42p each	00.84
4 toasting muffins	00.39
150g flaked almonds	01.39
500g sultanas	00.88
45g jar of cumin	00.49
18g pot mixed herbs	00.25
100g packet garam masala	00.60
150ml teriyaki sauce	01.00
100g whole hazelnuts	01.50
180g tahini	01.80
100g miso	01.50
coconut milk	00.59
200g packet egg replacer (e.g. Orgran)	03.25
2 x 300g tins of broad beans in water	00.80
500g dried green lentils	00.75
150g vegan Worcestershire Sauce	01.29
TOTAL	**£47.19**

Tight Budget Tian

A tian is a baking dish; like a casserole, the name of the dish is the same as the food it contains. Also like the casserole, it is a good-natured dish that will adapt to suit you and your purse. This is a pared-down version of a traditional tian, which usually has a sauce and a least three ingredients, but if you use lots of garlic and an intensely flavoured vegan cheddar, it is still a feast, albeit frugal. (It does need sides, though, which I have detailed below. It would be a good idea to start cooking the lentils for the salad before you start anything else). It looks pretty to match the circumference of the aubergine to those of the potatoes as closely as possible.

Ingredients

4 cloves of garlic
85g vegan margarine
115g extra mature vegan cheddar, finely grated
1 large aubergine
4 large potatoes

Method

1) Preheat the oven to Gas Mark 6/200°C/400°F.

2) Slice the potatoes into 2cm slices and boil for five minutes.

3) Melt the marg on a very low heat and slowly fry the garlic until translucent. Turn off the heat.

4) Slice the aubergine into 2cm slices.

5) In an oval dish, arrange the aubergine and potatoes in alternate slices.

6) Pour the garlic marg over the vegetables and sprinkle over the vegan cheese, then bake for 20 minutes.

Obviously this would not be enough to satiate a household of four, so I have put bread muffins in this week's shopping list to serve as a side, along with the ingredients to make a lentil salad: boil 200g green lentils for around 35 minutes, then combine with a finely chopped onion, two chopped apples and 2 tbs sultanas. It goes beautifully with this tian.

Treasure in the Tide

Batter is a thrifty classic, probably because it contains a good source of both protein and calcium, and if you get it right it has a wonderfully moreish crunch. If there is one lesson I have learnt about making batter, it is that you cannot skip the stage of getting its metal container almost smoking hot before pouring in the raw mixture, if you want crispness at the end. The genesis of this cross between Toad in the Hole and Vegetable Tempura was having a weakness for both! The vegetables reminded my children of jewels being washed onto the shore by the sea so they came up with this name.

Ingredients

350 ml soya milk
The equivalent of 4 eggs' worth egg replacer
250g plain flour
1 teaspoon baking powder
1 heaped teaspoon mixed herbs
½ teaspoon sea salt
400g cleaned button mushrooms, left whole
2 packets baby corn, washed and dried
1 tablespoon vegetable oil
Vegan Worcestershire sauce

Method

1) Preheat the oven to Gas Mark 7/220°C/430°F.

2) Whisk the soya milk and egg replacer together until you have a really bubbly batter. Add the flour, salt and herbs a little at a time, whisking all the time, until the batter is as smooth as possible. Add a few drops of Worcestershire sauce and whisk again.

3) Put the oil into a large metal dish and oven heat until it is almost smoking.

4) Have oven gloves, batter and vegetables at the ready. Taking great care, pour the batter into the hot tin and quickly add the vegetables, stirring speedily to distribute them fairly evenly in the batter, then pop the tin back in the oven as fast as you can. Cook for 40–45 minutes until the edges are dark brown and the middle is yellowy-brown, but firm — use a skewer to check, as you would for a cake.

Spaghetti Plus Three Sauces

(I recommend you read the recipe through before starting; a bit of fiddle-faddling, but worth it!)

Cherry tomatoes, baby beets and small spinach leaves, which are all easily available in early autumn — both in the supermarkets or in farmers' or street markets — have a more concentrated flavour than their full-grown counterparts, so they make the best sauces for spaghetti. If you serve the sauces on the side (either in little pots or on one side of the plate) diners can choose whether they want to mix the sauces or eat them separately.

The beetroot sauce here was inspired by the soup Borscht, which originated in the Ukraine but is popular in many other Eastern European countries.

This sweet vegetable is combined with a sour liquid, which is taste bud-tingling stuff; the same principle works by combining the tomato with lemon-infused coconut milk. A contrasting flavour and colour is then needed to balance the meal; the earthy/creamy spinach sauce does it to perfection.

You may be pleasantly surprised by the reaction to the purple sauce; roasting the beetroot intensifies its sweetness and makes it far more acceptable to avowed beetroot haters. There was a surprise conversion at my table anyway!

Ingredients

340g spaghetti

For the Roasted Beetroot Sauce

9 cooked baby beetroots, vacuum packed
30g vegan margarine
2 tablespoons olive oil

pinch of salt
A few grindings of black pepper
half of a 500ml pot of vegan yoghurt

For the Cherry Tomato and Coconut Lemon Sauce

500g cherry tomatoes, halved
2 cloves garlic, chopped finely
20g vegan margarine

1 tablespoon olive oil
1 lemon
1 tin of coconut milk

For the Creamy Spinach Sauce

1 small carton vegan cream (or half a large one, such as Elmlea)
1 200g pack washed organic young spinach

2 cloves garlic, chopped finely
30g vegan margarine

Method

1) Preheat oven to 180°C/350°F/Gas Mark 4.

2) Put a large pan of water on to boil for the spaghetti, then start with the tomato sauce: melt the margarine with the oil in small saucepan. Stir in the garlic, and gently heat for about three minutes. Put the tomatoes in a baking dish, then pour over the garlicky juices from the pan. Put the baby beetroots in another shallow baking dish, pour on the oil and margarine, then shake the pan to coat. Sprinkle with salt and pepper. Roast both beetroots and tomatoes for 15 minutes.

3) Once the water comes to boil, put in the spaghetti and cook for 11 minutes.

4) Tip a tin of coconut milk into the food processor, add the juice of a lemon and a little salt, then process with the roasted tomatoes until you have a pretty coral colour. Set aside and rinse out the bowl of the food processor in readiness for the beetroots.

5) Heat the margarine in a non-stick wok and cook the spinach with the garlic until wilted. Turn off the heat and beat in the vegan cream.

6) Process the roasted beetroot with the vegan yoghurt. (A little juggling is needed if the spaghetti water is ready too much in advance of the beetroot or vice versa. If the beetroot is ready first,

keep the vegetables in the oven but turn it off and cover the baby beetroot with foil. If the water is ready too soon, turn off the heat, cover the pan, then reheat the water when needed).

7) Reheat the sauces (very gently to prevent curdling) about 3 minutes before the end of the spaghetti's cooking time.

8) Drain the spaghetti thoroughly and serve the sauces alongside, either collectively or individually, depending on how much you or whoever is doing the washing up is prepared to deal with!

Ful Masala Style Broad Beans

Ful Masala, if you've never had the pleasure, is an African/Middle Eastern dish made with fava beans. You can get these tinned at supermarkets now, and I cook with them a lot, but as canned broad beans are cheaper and as I needed to stick within the budget I decided to see what the recipe was like with broad beans, which is the same bean anyway. This recipe was inspired by the Ful Masala I was served at an Ethiopian restaurant, with the addition of tomatoes which are still good in early autumn. This is great to make for a *crowd because it can be easily scaled up, when pennies allow, and is a lovely relaxed way of eating. This uses half a pack of vegan feta. Make double of this recipe, minus the pitta bread, if you intend to cook tomorrow's dish.

Ingredients

1 packet pitta
300g tin broad beans in water
4 cloves garlic, chopped fairly finely
1 teaspoon gram masala

2 teaspoons tomato puree
500g cherry tomatoes
Halved 100g vegan feta
55g vegan margarine

244

Method

1) Melt the margarine on a low light, then gently fry the garlic in a non-stick wok for one minute.

2) Add the tomatoes and gram masala. Fry until they begin to break down.

3) Add the beans. Gently stir and lift to combine with the tomatoes.

4) Simmer the sauce while you toast the pitta.

5) Slowly stirring the sauce occasionally, cut the pitta into strips and grate the rest of the vegan feta.

6) In each bowl, serve a portion of sauce topped with grated feta and surrounded by strips of pitta with which to scoop it up.

*It is also the perfect blueprint to which almost anything can be added if you find yourself with an unexpected guest to feed. Peppers or tinned tomatoes can pad out fresh tomatoes if you're short; a can of butter beans stretches insufficient broad beans; creamed corn will preserve the richness of the sauce if your marg has run out and any vegan cheese may be used to mix in with the grated feta.

(If you keep the vegetables to beans; creamy sauce to spices and garlic to cheese ratios roughly the same as above, it is virtually foolproof). I have used all of these substitutions/additions on many occasions after receiving a text beginning, "Is it alright if I invite...?"

Ful Masala Over Rosemary Infused Mash

This gives the Ful Masala Style Broad Beans another outing – they are too good to be served only one way!

Ingredients

600g organic potatoes
60g vegan margarine
2 tablespoons plant milk
Fresh rosemary leaves, stripped from the stalk using your thumb and forefinger

1 red chilli, plus half of yesterday's bean mixture (if you didn't cook it, follow the recipe for Ful Masala Style Broad Beans, stirring in the vegan cheese, but omit the pitta bread.)

Method

1) Preheat the oven to Gas Mark 6/200°C/400°F. Prepare the bean mixture if necessary.

2) Boil the potatoes for 20 minutes or so until tender.

3) In the meantime, melt the margarine, gently fry the chilli until tender, remove with a slotted spoon, then stir in the rosemary. Set aside until the potatoes are ready.

4) Mash the potatoes with the plant milk and stir in the chilli. Set aside.

5) Put the broad bean mixture into the bottom of a shallow casserole dish. Holding a sieve over the mashed potatoes to catch the spiky rosemary leaves, pour the melted margarine into the potatoes and mix in with a wooden spoon. (It is amazing how quickly the margarine absorbs the rosemary flavour, so do not fear that it won't be sufficiently infused after such a short time).

6) Smooth the potatoes over the Ful Masala and fork it up.

7) Bake for 20 minutes.

Autumn Pie: Two Potato Bobotie

This celebrates the colours, flavours and joys of autumn. The mixture of earthy and sweet potatoes is El Dorado for mash lovers. Bobotie is a famous South African mince dish (substituted with green lentils here) which usually has a slightly eggy topping which I replaced with potatoes. Another one of the win-win joys of fusion cooking: you get to keep all your favourite parts as well as adding beloved foods for good measure.

Ingredients

170g sweet potatoes, halved or quartered, depending on size

300g organic potatoes good for mashing, such as Maris Piper, halved or quartered as above

2 tablespoons plant milk

2 onions, chopped

2 apples, chopped

40g vegan margarine (or more if you like creamy mash)

1 teaspoon garam masala

1 teaspoon cumin

250g dried green lentils

2 tablespoons mango chutney

1 tablespoon flaked almonds

2 heaped tablespoons sultanas

A little oil

Method

1) Wash the green lentils, discarding any stones, then boil for 35–40 minutes until just tender (reserve a little bite). When they've been boiling for about 20 minutes, put the water on the boil for the two types of potatoes. Boil the potatoes and sweet potatoes in two pots, each for 15–20 minutes, depending on size, until tender.

2) Mash the two types of potato separately, with 20g margarine and a tablespoon of plant milk in each. Combine the two, but roughly; you don't want the colours to meld together.

3) Preheat the oven to Gas Mark 6/200°C/400°F.

4) Gently fry the onion and apple in a little oil together in a non-stick wok for ten minutes to release their sweetness. Stir in the garam masala and cumin and cook for another 3 minutes, still on a low light.

5) Tip in the cooked lentils, chutney, almonds and sultanas and cook gently for 10 minutes. Tip it all into the bottom of an ovenproof dish.

6) Put the mixed potato mash in a piping bag fitted with a star nozzle.

7) Pipe the potato over the filling; if you haven't over-mixed the two potatoes, you should get a lovely stripy effect. Alternatively, if you don't fancy piping, you could just swirl the colours together with the tip of a large spoon to marble them.

8) Cook for 15 minutes, until only slightly browned, in order to reheat the potatoes while retaining the orange glow.

Lemony Pitta Hazelnut Loaf with Miso and Tahini Sauce

This loaf starts life in Britain then travels to the Middle and Far East, and its sauce travels in the same direction. Nut loaves are not an exact science but they do need some experimentation. They can fall apart when too wet, or stay together well but are too dry and heavy (and they do still have a bit of a 1970s hippy reputation). But a good nut roast is such a useful addition to your thrifty repertoire; once you find a wet/dry ingredients ratio that works for you, you can use all your favourite available tastes and combinations. The key is to have a mixture which is soft but not wet. Such a consistency will produce a moist but sliceable loaf, and to achieve this, all you need to do is to keep checking how well the dry ingredients are soaking up the wet, which is not difficult if you add the latter gradually.

Ingredients

For the Lemony Pitta Hazelnut Loaf

100g packet blanched hazelnuts

2 cloves garlic, chopped very finely

1 tablespoon olive oil

4 spring onions, green parts removed, chopped finely

8 cherry tomatoes, halved

125g mixed exotic mushrooms, chopped roughly

2 pitta breads, whizzed into breadcrumbs in the food processor

1small pack of fresh coriander (28–31g), chopped. Reserve a couple of sprigs for the sauce.

2 Lemons (juice and zest of one lemon, juice from half of the other lemon and slices from its remaining half for garnish)

3 tablespoons Teriyaki sauce

freshly ground pepper

For Miso and Tahini Sauce

25g vegan margarine

25g flour

1 pint (500ml) plant milk

2 teaspoon tahini

2 sprigs coriander, chopped (see above)

1 heaped tablespoon miso

Freshly ground pepper pinch sea salt

Method

1) Preheat the oven to Gas Mark 6/200°C/400°F. Very thoroughly grease a 450g/1 1b loaf tin or silicone mould.

2) Fry the onion very gently until transparent.

3) Add the mushrooms, tomato, garlic and coriander, and fry on a low light for about 5–7 minutes, until the mushrooms are tender but still firm. You don't want the tomatoes to completely disintegrate either.

4) Divide the hazelnuts into two halves. Roughly chop one half and leave the rest whole. Add both to the above mixture.

5) Transfer this mixture into a big bowl, then add the pitta crumbs and lemon zest.

6) Mix the lemon juice and Teriyaki sauce together, then gradually add to the mixture in the bowl. If it looks very dry, add a little water. Grind some pepper into the mix.

7) Spoon the mixture into your prepared tin/mould then press it down until it is very flat and compacted.

8) Bake for about 40–45 minutes, until the hazelnuts are golden brown and the loaf is set. Leave to cool slightly (say ten minutes) before you turn it out.

9) As it cools, make the sauce: melt the margarine, add the flour and blend until you have a paste. Cook for about five minutes, then turn off the heat. Gradually add the plant milk, until you have a smooth sauce, then bring to the boil. Simmer gently, then add the tahini and reserved coriander. Stir well until the tahini is well blended. Turn the heat off, then add the miso. Stir again, add a grinding of pepper and a pinch of sea salt then transfer to a jug or gravy boat.

10) Turn out your nut roast and garnish with the lemon slices you have set aside. Serve with the Miso and Tahini Sauce.

Suggestions and Shopping List for Breakfasts and Lunches for Autumn, Week One

BREAKFASTS

Pear Porridge

Overnight Sultana and Blackberry Oats

Caramelised Onion on Crumpets

Baked beans with Cumin on Toast

Wheat Biscuits with Sultanas

Bircher-style Muesli with Apples and Strawberry Yoghurt

The Full Celtic

LUNCHES

Wraps with Tahini Roasted Sweet Potatoes and Worcestershire Lentils

Pear and Peanut Butter Sandwiches

Wraps with Red Pepper Hummus, Spring Onions and lettuce

Bombay Potato Salad Lettuce Wraps

Sweet Potato Rosti

Sausage and Mango Chutney Rolls

Nut Roast Rolls

Shopping List

6 crumpets	00.35
2 x 4 large brown rolls	00.98
2 x 410g baked beans	00.46
170g red pepper hummus	00.69
1 kg porridge oats	00.75
1.5 kg organic potatoes	01.39
568ml cider	00.85
24 wheat biscuits	00.69
2 packets of 6 veggie sausages	04.00
600g pears	01.35
Round lettuce	00.40
250g cherry tomatoes	00.53
8 tortilla wraps	00.99
340g crunchy peanut butter	00.65
454g strawberry jam	00.29
800g bread	00.50
1 packet vegan bacon	02.00
25g parsley	00.50
125g blackberries	01.49
(or free if you're lucky!)	
TOTAL	**£17.71**
DINNERS	**£47.19**
TOTAL WITH DINNERS	**£64.90**

Already accounted for: sultanas, teriyaki sauce, onions, mango chutney, cumin, Worcestershire sauce, sweet potatoes, yoghurt, margarine, flour, and apples.

Notes on Breakfasts and Lunches for Autumn, Week One

Pear Porridge
Add a cored, chopped pear to each bowl of porridge.

Overnight Sultana and Blackberry Oats
Let the sultanas soak with the oats to plump them up but add the fresh blackberries in the morning so they are perky and fresh.

Caramelised Onion on Crumpets
Very, very slowly, fry four sliced onions with a teaspoon of sugar for at least ten minutes until they are soft and brown. Pile onto toasted crumpets and enjoy the sweetness!

Baked Beans with Cumin on Toast
As you are warming two tins of baked beans, add a teaspoon of cumin for extra spice and nutrition.

Wheat Biscuits with Sultanas (start the night before)
Soak the sultanas overnight to get the most from them. Drain thoroughly in the morning.

Bircher-Style Museli with Strawberry Yoghurt (start the night before)
To the 250ml of yoghurt which remains to you after that used for the Roasted Beetroot Sauce, whisk in 3 tablespoons strawberry jam until thoroughly combined. Add 4 finely chopped apples (they will be left over from those bought from the Bobotie Pie) and 2 tablespoons oats. Mix thoroughly and leave overnight before dividing into bowls in the morning.

The Full Celtic
Please see at the end of the notes.

Wraps with Tahini Roasted Sweet Potatoes and Worcestershire Lentils (not one for early in the morning so prepare the filling the night before if you wish)
Preheat the oven to Gas Mark6/200°C/400°F. Take the 300g sweet potatoes left over from the Two Potato Pie, scrub them well, then cut into wedges. Slightly thin 2 tablespoons tahini with a little water, then roll the potatoes around in this until they are thoroughly covered. Put in a shallow baking dish and roast for around 30–40 minutes until they

are soft in the middle and crispy on the outside. This will give you time to boil and drain 4 heaped tablespoons green lentils (usually only takes about 30 minutes). Add 1 tablespoon of vegan Worcestershire Sauce to the hot lentils, stir thoroughly, and allow to cool. Combine the lentils with the sweet potatoes, then happily stuff your wraps.

Pear and Peanut Butter Sandwiches
Mix ½ chopped pear thoroughly with every 1 tablespoon peanut butter (which is roughly what you would need per sandwich) to prevent it going brown before you start spreading.

Wraps with Red Pepper Hummus, Spring Onions and Lettuce
(save half for later in the week).
Put the lettuce in first, mix the onions and hummus together then pop it on top of the lettuce. Chop the 2 spring onions well, or it will be a bit too acidic and difficult to eat!

Bombay Potato Salad Lettuce Wraps
(not one for a busy, time-pressed morning, but the filling can be made the night before and stored in the fridge).
Peel, chop and steam 750g of potatoes. While still warm, add 2 tablespoons sultanas, 1 tablespoon mango chutney and 1 teaspoon cumin. Mix well, then serve in lettuce wraps (from the other half of the round lettuce).

Sweet Potato Rosti
Grate the remaining 330g of sweet potato finely. Mix with two grated onions. Put in a tea towel and squeeze thoroughly so minimal liquid remains. Add salt and pepper, then add flattened tablespoons to a non-stick pan coated with vegetable oil. Fry until crispy on the outside and tender in the middle. Serve with some sliced baby beetroots (leftover from the Spaghetti with Three Sauces).

Sausage and Mango Chutney Rolls
Bake or grill 2 sausages per person, slice vertically, then serve with some mango chutney in rolls. (In the two packets of six veggie sausages bought this week, 4 will go in The Full Celtic and 8 in these rolls).

Nut Roast Rolls
Leftover Lemony Pitta Hazelnut Loaf, sliced thinly, makes a good roll filling.

The Full Celtic

(Scottish Potato Pancakes, Sweet Potato Irish Coddle, Welsh Rarebit Tomatoes)

This is a great leisurely feast to make if you love a full cooked breakfast but find the red-faced racing from hob to hob a little stressful; the coddle can be cooked in the oven and the tomatoes can simmer gently while you fry the pancakes. Tweaking the traditional coddle by using sweet potatoes makes it lighter – it will be too heavy with the potato pancakes otherwise. The coddle could be made the night before and reheated for 20 minutes in a preheated oven at Gas Mark 6/200°C/400°F.

Ingredients

For the Coddle
200g sweet potatoes
1 large onion, diced
1 vegan bacon rasher
4 vegan sausages
1 tablespoon olive oil
1 large onion, diced
1 cloves garlic, chopped finely
250ml cider
250ml vegetable stock, made with a stock cube
1 small packet parsley, roughly chopped

For the Tomatoes
250g cherry tomatoes, halved
1 tablespoon vegan Worcestershire Sauce
85g vegan Cheddar, grated

For the Potato Pancakes
450g organic potatoes, cut into uniform sizes
60g plain flour
½ teaspoon salt
60g vegan margarine
1 tablespoon plant milk of choice

Method

1) Start with the coddle. Preheat the oven to Gas Mark 6/200°C/400°F. Make the stock by dissolving one stock cube in 250ml boiling water.

2) Peel the sweet potatoes and cut them into 2cm cubes. Set aside while you lightly fry the onions for three minutes. This is just to release their natural sweetness – you don't have to wait until they are translucent. Scrape the onion into a casserole dish, then use the same pan to quickly fry the sausages for 2 minutes only (you simply want to brown them) and slice into coins. In the meantime, chop the bacon. Add both to the casserole dish and mix. Tip in the garlic, sweet potatoes, cider and stock, cover the casserole dish, then put into the oven for one hour.

3)   Meanwhile, peel the potatoes for the pancakes if you are not using a ricer. Boil them until they are tender for about 20 minutes, or less if you cut them small. Mash (or put through the ricer), then add 30g of the margarine, the plant milk and the flour. Beat vigorously, then when the mixture is cold, shape into a ball with floured hands, flatten it, then roll it out to 2cm thickness and cut out your preferred shapes with a biscuit cutter.

4)   Five minutes before the coddle is ready, combine the vegan cheese with the Worcestershire sauce, then, stirring now and then, simmer gently on the hob with the tomatoes until the tomatoes are softened and the cheese has melted.

5)   Melt the rest of the margarine for the pancakes, then fry for approximately two minutes on each side on a high heat to produce a gorgeous crust.

6)   On a large plate, dish out the coddle, top with the tomatoes and the parsley, then surround the whole with your pancakes. Feast away!

*Chippa is a good vegan brand. You can buy it at ASDA for 1.29 at the time of writing. Life is another one which you can get in whole food shops, but it is more expensive.

Dinners for Autumn, Week Two

1. Tomatican Wraps in a Mushroom Cream Sauce

2. Freeform Bipbimbap

3. Slightly Spiced Rough Root Mash with Sausages

4. Stuffed Paired Pears on a Bed of Red Onion Rice

5. October Vegetable Curry

6. Jackets Stuffed with October Vegetable Curry

7. Rice Balls in Walnut Sauce with Vegetable Bravas

Shopping List for Dinners for Autumn, Week Two

	Prices
Vegetables/Fruit	
2 x 1.5kg organic potatoes at £1.39 each	02.78
31g fresh parsley	00.69
2 x 200g button mushrooms at 85p each	01.70
one cucumber	00.49
250g radishes	00.53
one head of celery	00.53
135g baby corn	00.95
one lemon	00.29
2 avocados	01.65
6 oranges	00.99
31g fresh parsley	00.69
400g green beans	01.50
500g carrots and swede	01.50
440g beansprouts	00.65
500g pears	00.90
550g parsnips	00.50
1 kg brown onions	00.59
a large swede	00.50
2 red onions	00.24
250g cherry tomatoes	00.58
300g strawberries	01.09
2 x 500g organic carrots at 58p each	01.16
Fridge	
250g vegan margarine	00.85
1 litre plant milk	00.59
250ml oat cream	00.75
170g vegan cream cheese	01.80
2 x 500g vegan yoghurt	03.00
349g extra firm tofu	1.25

Cupboard

2 x tins of chopped tomatoes at 34p each	00.68
45g cumin	00.49
50g paprika	00.49
1 kg brown basmati rice	01.35
2 tins of 400g chickpeas at 33p each	00.66
50g jar of paprika	00.49
500g pack of icing sugar	00.75
170g chipotle sauce	01.00
350ml white wine vinegar	00.75
150ml teriyaki sauce	01.50
250ml sesame oil	01.60
250ml walnut oil	01.60
27g chilli flakes	01.00
283g own brand Tikka mild curry paste	01.00
200g chopped mixed nuts	01.20
3 400g coconut milk at 59p each (Caribbean Choice)	01.77
411g peaches in juice	00.33
*8 tortilla wraps	00.89
2 x 130g walnuts at £1.29 each	02.58
18g dried mixed herbs	00.25
310g pitted green olives in a jar	00.69
75g packet mini pappadums	01.00
525g packet vegan custard	00.87
100g vegetarian jelly	00.80
325g tin budget sweetcorn in water	00.35
250g sesame seeds	01.09

Freezer

907g frozen pea	00.69
2 x 6 vegan sausages (varies; whichever on special)	03.00
TOTAL	**£55.83**

* From an 8 wrap packet, you'll be using one and half wraps per person for the Tomatican (=6) and making breadcrumbs for the Rice Balls with the remaining 2 wraps

Already accounted for: porridge oats, garlic, chilli, mixed herbs, soy sauce, vegan Worcestershire sauce, tomato puree, breadcrumbs (from the tortilla wraps frozen from last week).

Tomatican Wraps in a Mushroom Cream Sauce

Tomatican is a Chilean stew with a concentrated tomato flavour. It is mostly served with fried potatoes but I have omitted them only because it would be too heavy as well as the wrap and the mushroom sauce. It is also usually made with fresh tomatoes, but as they are tailing off this time of year canned are fine, with chipotle sauce, a smoked chilli sauce popular in Chile (and everywhere else now)! This concentrates the tomato flavour and eradicates any possible tinny flavour. There are multiple layers of flavour here (smoky, creamy, spicy, tangy) but the end result is definitely greater than the sum of its parts.

Ingredients

Wrapping
4 tortillas (there are usually six in a packet – we'll be using the other two on Day 7; freeze these until needed)

Tomatican
325g tin of sweetcorn
200g green beans, topped, tailed and cut into 2cm lengths
4 medium onions, finely chopped
4 cloves garlic, finely chopped
1 tablespoon olive oil
2 x 400g chopped tomatoes
1 30g packet fresh parsley, finely chopped
1 teaspoon cumin
1 teaspoon paprika
2 teaspoon teaspoon chipotle sauce

Mushroom Sauce
1 teaspoon olive oil
400g button mushrooms, sliced thinly
2 tablespoons cider vinegar
145ml vegetable stock, made with one dissolved stock cube in water
125ml soya cream
1 garlic clove, chopped finely

Method

1) Preheat the oven to 200°C/400°F/Gas Mark 6. Put the water on to boil for the sweetcorn and beans and on the lowest possible light, fry the onion in the oil in a non-stick pan, turning frequently until translucent, for about ten minutes. Add the garlic and fry for another 3 minutes, then add all the rest of the ingredients and simmer gently for 20 minutes. In the meantime, boil the beans for ten minutes, drain the sweetcorn and add both to the stew; they'll only need another five minutes in the simmering stew.

2) Start the mushroom sauce about 10 minutes before the end of the Tomatican's simmering time. Heat the oil slightly in a non-stick wok or frying pan, add the mushrooms and turn them gently until they are tender (about 5 minutes). Add the cider vinegar, garlic, stock and soya cream and bring to the boil. Cook, stirring all the time, for 2 minutes, until the sauce has slightly thickened. Don't expect a thick sauce; as you can see from the photo, it is quite fluid, which is what you want so that you can drizzle it all over the wraps. Set aside, and cover.

3) Stuff the wraps with the Tomatican by putting them in a baking dish with their edges pointing towards you; spoon the sauce evenly between the six wraps, then pull the edges tightly over each other. Gently roll each one over (or not if it proves too awkward – it depends on how much wriggle room you have in your baking dish).

4) Bake the wraps for 5 minutes just to brown them, reheat the mushroom sauce gently, then serve the wraps with the sauce cascading over them.

Freeform Bibimbap

There are endless variations on this dish in Korea; it really depends on what is available and which vegetables and seasonings are the cook's (or friends' and family's) favourites, which makes sense when you hear that 'bibimbap' literally translates as 'mixed rice'. You can guarantee it will contain rice, vegetables, and one or more salty condiment (often doenjang), plus a paste or sauce with chilli. I haven't found doenjang in my local supermarket, but you can usually find it in shops which stock South East Asian ingredients. I have used teriyaki sauce for my salty condiment of choice, but as salt famously brings out the taste of vegetables, you can choose whichever savoury condiment is your favourite. If you are new to this dish, the idea is that, just before eating, the rice is mixed with all its accompaniments using chopsticks.

You may have to stem the enthusiasm of children a bit if you don't want it up the walls.

Ingredients

340g brown rice

200g green beans, topped and tailed and boiled for ten minutes before you begin (leave them in iced water until you are ready to use them; this stops the cooking process and retains the vibrant green)

1 large packet of bean sprouts

Half a cucumber

1 bunch or packet of radishes (roughly 200g, depending on the supermarket)

4 tablespoons teriyaki sauce

100g packet sesame seeds

4 carrots

2 sticks of celery

1 packet of baby corn (varies from supermarket to supermarket; aim for one around the 200g mark)

1 red chilli

½ teaspoon chilli flakes 2 cloves garlic

1 tablespoon sunflower oil (for the stir-frying)

2 teaspoon sesame oil

1 tablespoon walnut oil

Method

This recipe requires you to multi-multi task, but you can at least get a lot of it ready before you run around like some hysterical chef.

1) Put the water for the rice on to boil while you prepare the remaining vegetables (or just get them out of their packets if appropriate).

2) Top and tail the carrots and radishes. Cut the carrots into batons and do the same with the celery and cucumber. Cut the radishes into halves or quarters, depending on their size. Half the baby corn lengthways. Chop the chilli fairly finely and the garlic very finely. (Keep the two cloves separately on a big plate).

3) Put the rice on to boil (should take about 25 minutes, but check the instructions on the packet). Grease a medium-sized pudding basin.

4) While it is cooking, mix the cucumber with the chilli flakes and set aside. Leave the celery plain, but cover it.

5) Get out a wok and a frying pan, or two woks if you have them. In one pan, stir fry the baby corn on a high heat until just starting to soften (about 4 minutes), then add the 2 tablespoons teriyaki sauce and fry for another minute. Do the same in the other pan with the carrots and the other 2 tablespoons of oil and remaining 2 tablespoons teriyaki sauce, alternating between the two, so you keep both going with your wooden spoon.

6) Turn off the heat under both, transfer the vegetables to two plates and cover with foil.

7) Wipe out both pans with kitchen paper, drain the beans, then use one pan to stir-fry half of the beans in 1 teaspoon sesame oil, and the other to do the same with the radishes. Add one chopped chilli and the chopped clove of garlic to the beans. Add the remaining clove of garlic and the sesame seeds to the radishes. Stir fry both for five minutes; you will need to keep adjusting the heat as sesame oil retains its own heat fiercely – you may have to turn it off at some points.

8) Turn off the heat and keep both warm under two layers of foil.

9) Drain the rice and put it in your greased pudding basin. Push the rice down into the basin with your knuckles until it is densely compacted. Add a weight (I use a large, clean stone) and push down again.

10) Leave it for two minutes while you stir-fry the remaining green beans with the beans sprouts in the walnut oil for one minute. Add the garlic, salt and fry for another minute. If you don't have another pan or wok, you can do this quite successfully in a large saucepan, providing you keep things moving.

11) Turn out the rice on the flattest plate you have, then surround the mould with its vegetable accompaniments.

Slightly Spiced Rough Root Mash with Sausages

This was inspired by a favourite South Indian dish: dosai pancakes filed with lightly spiced, roughly mashed potatoes and carrots. In the interests of frugality, however, the spices are provided by the jar of curry paste which you can use again in this week's curry. This will serve four, so if you are making it just for yourself you could keep the rest of the sausages in the freezer and keep the remainder of the mash in the fridge for the following day. You could then combine it with some mashed tinned chickpeas (they cost about 33p) and shape them into veggie burgers with your hands, freezing what you don't use or having veggie burgers two days running.

Ingredients

12 medium potatoes
¼ large swede, cubed
4 large carrots, cubed
1 teaspoon curry paste
55g vegan margarine
8 sausages

Method

1) Peel the potatoes, cut into four and boil for 15–20 minutes until soft.

2) Simultaneously boil the carrots and swede for 10–13 minutes.

3) While these are simmering away, grill the sausages until cooked throughout.

4) Mash the cooked potatoes with the marg, then vigorously mix in the teaspoon of curry paste. A very light spicing is what works here.

5) Add the carrots and swede, then roughly mash them in with a fork; don't over mash to a puree – you don't want baby food.

6) Serve with the sausages a la Desperate Dan, with the sausages poking out of the mash.

Stuffed Paired Pears on a Bed of Red Onion Rice

Like many people, in my pre-vegan days, I would put pears on a cheese board, and still do that now so many great vegan cheeses are appearing. I thought it was about time I switched things up and gave the pears a lead role instead of a supporting one, and was happy I did! If you have children in the house who dislike the texture or taste of avocados, you could happily use just sweet pears.

Ingredients

240g rice
2 red onions
1 tbs olive oil
2 large pears, Comice if available
2 ripe avocados

8 heaped teaspoon vegan cream cheese
1 100g packet of chopped mixed nuts
juice of one lemon
1 finely chopped clove of garlic
4 cherry tomatoes

Method

1) Begin by getting the rice ready: boil 240g according to the instructions (usually 20–25 minutes). In the meantime, follow steps 2 to 5.

2) Spoon the cheese into a large bowl and thoroughly mix in the nuts.

3) Slice each avocado in half (the easiest way to do this is to find the middle and use the point of your knife to cut a clear line horizontally around the perimeter of the pear). Sprinkle with half the lemon juice.

4) Slice the Comice pears in half, keeping the stalk if you can, and gently remove the core with the tip of your knife. Sprinkle with the other half of the lemon juice.

5) Fill the cavities with the nutty cheesy mixture and garnish each portion with half a cherry tomato.

6) When the rice is cooked, gently fry the red onion with the olive oil, and mix into the rice.

7) Serve the pears on the bed of rice.

OCTOBER VEGETABLE CURRY WITH ACCOMPANIMENTS

Mini Pappadums, Radish Raita, Peach and Orange Lassi

Dessert: Trifles in Oranges

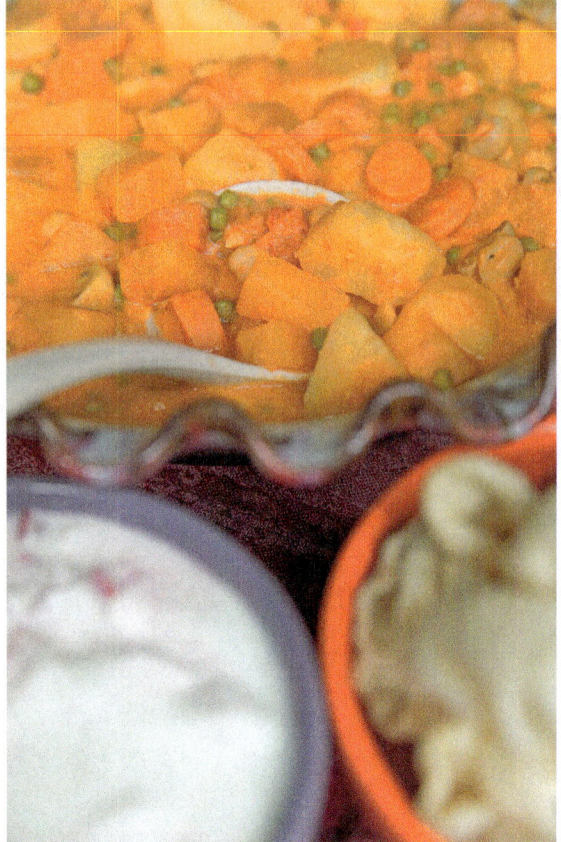

Curry powder is one of the oldest examples of a fusion ingredient, with not the happiest of beginnings, as its origins were based in the British colonisation of India in the eighteenth century. The spice mix was developed after the British developed a taste for Indian spices and wanted to take them home. Anglo/Indian curries are now a common feature in home menus. This one uses a paste because a jar of curry paste keeps in the fridge for a long time and is incredibly thrifty and useful, and it doesn't have the powdery aftertaste you sometimes get from cheap spice mixes.

This makes a huge pot of sumptuous, creamy curry, glowing with autumnal colours, enough for a complete meal and plenty to be served with jacket potatoes the following day. You do need a big pot, such as a stockpot. You can get them for as little as seven pounds on EBay, but if that's out the question, you can use two saucepans.

NB: The accompaniments are entirely up to you of course, but if you do want to make them, put the coconut milk for the dessert in the fridge the night before. Also, you need to make the raita before you begin the curry so the flavours can develop.

October Vegetable Curry

Ingredients

4 cloves garlic, chopped into tiny pieces
500g onions, chopped finely
2tablespoons oil
4 large organic carrots, sliced into discs
500g potatoes, cut into chunks
1 large parsnip, cut into chunks
Half of one large swede, cut into large dice
4 tablespoons frozen peas
1 tin chickpeas
2 tins chopped tomatoes
2 tins coconut milk
4 tablespoons tomato puree
2 teaspoon mild curry paste (more of less according to taste) salt and pepper

Method

This is a recipe which really benefits from vigilant testing of the ingredients; underdone root vegetables ruin it. I have found that it is better to start with precooked potatoes, swede, carrots and parsnips, otherwise it takes forever to cook. They also absorb the flavours of the sauce more efficiently if they are tender to start with.

1) Boil or steam the carrots, potatoes, swede and parsnips. 20 minutes should be okay for all of them, but there could be variation, so it is better to cook them on all four rings and check each pot after 15 minutes. Sometimes carrots and swede can take longer, up to 25 minutes, so keep checking. (Of course, if you have a tiered steamer, you will need fewer rings).

2) Fry the onions until tender in the oil.

3) Add curry paste to the softened onions, mix well and cook until completely soft.

4) Add the tomato puree, tomatoes, peas, coconut milk and chickpeas. Stir well, then add a little hot water to each emptied coconut milk and tomato tin, swirling it around to lift off the liquid, then pour it in the pot too. (If you add too much water, you'll lose the creaminess of the curry).

5) Tip in the cooked vegetables and give it a thorough, but gentle, stir.

6) Add the chopped garlic, then simmer on a very low light for 5 minutes.

7) Add salt and pepper to your taste, checking to see if you have it right – it is a large pot to season. You may even wish to add more curry paste if family members like it hot. Or, if tastes vary and you can be bothered with the faff, add different seasonings to each portion, reheating gently afterwards.

8) Serve today's four portions with peach and orange lassi, mini pappadums and radish or celery raita (see overleaf).

9) Serve tomorrow's portion with a large jacket potato each.

Peach and Orange Lassi

Cut 4 oranges in half, then remove the contents using a sharp knife to cut the segments away from the pith. Scoop out the flesh with a teaspoon. Be careful not to pierce the skin if you want to make this week's trifles. Put the orange peel "cups" face down on a plate in the fridge. Remove any pith from the segments, then roughly chop them and discard any pips. Process the orange flesh with the tin of peaches (including juice) and a half a 500g carton of vegan yoghurt.

Radish Raita

Top and tail your radishes, mix with the other half of the carton of yoghurt and two chopped garlic cloves, then leave the flavours to infuse for at least half an hour. If you prefer, you can use 4 finely chopped sticks of celery instead.

Trifles in Oranges (Begin the Night Before)

1) Put a tin of coconut milk in the fridge overnight to allow the cream to separate and solidify.

2) When you begin the trifles, make up some jelly according to the instructions on the packet, then pour into your 8 pre-prepared orange cups, about a third of the way up. Allow to set in the fridge (doesn't take long with vegan jelly).

3) Follow with a layer of vegan custard, reserving 3 tablespoons for the coconut cream, then top with *coconut cream and a strawberry.

*To make the coconut cream, remove the coconut milk from the fridge and spoon out the separated cream into a bowl. Beat in the reserved custard and enough icing sugar for the cream to hold its shape.

Rice Balls in Walnut Sauce with Vegetable Bravas

This is a dish for those days when you can devote a couple of hours to cooking. Having said that, a lot could be prepared in advance, even the day before: the walnut sauce isn't cooked, so that may be made beforehand to allow the flavours to develop for up 24 hours before serving – allow it to come to room temperature after removing from the fridge though; the Vegetable Bravas can be made a day beforehand and reheated gently; the rice balls happily sit in the fridge for a couple of days, or you can freeze them without any loss of flavour. The majority of supermarkets sell walnuts in 100g or 200g packets, but if your local one doesn't, you can also buy them at Boots and Poundland, if you don't want to be left with any spare nuts from larger packets.

NB: You'll need breadcrumbs. If you haven't frozen the two spare tortilla wraps from the beginning of the week, you'll need to process the ends of a loaf of bread.

Ingredients

Walnut Sauce
200g walnuts (packets of pieces are usually cheaper)
500g soya yoghurt
2 cloves garlic
1 tablespoons tomato puree

Rice Balls
349g block firm tofu
2 tablespoon porridge oats
120 ml water
2 tablespoons fresh parsley

10 green olives in brine, drained and chopped small

1 celery stalk, finely chopped

70g brown rice

50g breadcrumbs (from 2 tortilla wraps reserved in the freezer; see above)

salt to taste (you may not need it, as the olives will taste salty)

2 cloves garlic, chopped finely

1 onion, finely chopped

another 50g breadcrumbs to coat (there should be enough from the reserved wraps, otherwise you could use the end of a loaf)

Vegetable Bravas

¼ one large swede, chopped into large chunks

2 organic carrots, sliced

Sauce:

1 tablespoon olive oil

½ teaspoon paprika

1 clove garlic, finely chopped

salt to taste

Method

1) Remove the two reserved tortilla wraps from the freezer (or bread for 50g breadcrumbs). Boil the rice according to the instructions on the packet (usually about 25 minutes) then set it aside, because the rice needs to be cooked and cooled for this recipe.

2) Mix together the ingredients for the Bravas sauce; set aside. (Put it in the fridge if making in advance).

3) Finely chop the walnuts for the other sauce in the food processor. Add the tomato puree, garlic and yoghurt, stir until thoroughly combined, then set aside. (As above, if not using immediately, put it in the fridge. NB: Both sauces need to come to room temperature before serving.

4) Before beginning the rice balls, grease a baking sheet and preheat the oven to Gas Mark 6/200°/400°F.

5) To make the rice balls, blend the tofu, water, porridge oats, soy sauce and parsley until you have a thick paste. Make your breadcrumbs in the food processor.

6) In a large bowl, combine the breadcrumbs, olives, celery, onion, garlic and cooled rice, then add the paste to this mixture and mix really well with a spatula, making sure you reach the bottom and sides of the bowl. What you are after here is both moistness and firmness. If it seems a little dry, add a drop more water or lemon juice. If it seems too sloppy, process another slice of bread and gradually add the crumbs to the mixture. (The water content of tofu and vegetables vary, so you do need to use your judgement here; if the mixture is too wet, it will be difficult to roll it into balls. Conversely, a dry mixture will not be rescued by the sauce, so be

cautious). Shape the mixture into the balls somewhere between the size of a ping-pong ball and a tennis ball. With luck, it should make about 16 balls, four for each person.

7) Spread the breadcrumbs over a large plate or board. Roll the balls into the breadcrumbs, using the flat of your hand, until they are completely coated.

8) Cook for 20 minutes (check after 15) until well browned. Keep these until foil under the Vegetable Bravas is ready.

9) While the rice balls are in the oven, put two pans water of on to boil. Remove sauces from the fridge.

10) Cook the carrots and swede for roughly tender minutes, until tender.

11) Pour the yoghurt sauce over the rice balls and drizzle the Bravas sauce over the hot vegetables. Serve immediately, savouring each taste and texture.

Suggestions and Shopping List for Breakfasts and Lunches for Autumn, Week Two

BREAKFASTS

Cornflakes with Strawberries

Wheat Biscuits with Oranges

Herbed Baked Beans on toast

Cornflakes with Sultanas

Wheat Biscuits with Strawberries

Muffins with Marmalade

Pitta Bread Stuffed with Sausage Rice

LUNCHES

Rolls with Cucumber, Celery and Homemade Caramelised Onion Hummus

Rolls with Peanut Butter and Finely Chopped Celery

Wraps Filled with Chickpeas Smashed with Worcestershire Sauce and Sliced Olives

Pittas filled with Grated Carrot, Chopped Nuts and Chipotle Cream Cheese

Peanut Butter and Marmalade Sandwiches

Wraps Filled with Baby Corn, Peanuts and Tomatoes Splashed with Soy Sauce

Herby Scones and Chipotle Hummus

Shopping List

2 x own brand baked beans	00.46
4 muffins	00.39
2 x 6 pitta bread at 42p each	00.84
135g baby corn	00.95
6 tomatoes	00.59
8 large brown rolls at 45p for four	00.90
One lemon	00.25
1 800g loaf brown bread	00.50
500g own brand cornflakes	00.38
454g marmalade	00.27
340g peanut butter	00.65
500g dried chickpeas	00.75
200g peanuts	00.48
8 tortilla wraps	00.89
TOTAL	**£08.30**
DINNERS	**£55.83**
TOTAL WITH DINNERS	**£64.13**

Already accounted for: wheat biscuits, Worcestershire sauce, walnut oil, soy sauce, chipotle paste, dried mixed herbs, olives, strawberries, oranges, sultanas, tahini, cucumber, celery, flour, baking powder and rice.

Notes on Breakfasts and Lunches for Autumn, Week Two

Cornflakes with Strawberries and Wheat Biscuits with Strawberries
There will be strawberries left over from the mini trifles. It is better to add some chopped strawberries to your breakfast at the end to prevent mushiness to either the fruit or the cereal.

Wheat Biscuits with Oranges
There will be 2 oranges left over this week. It is a pleasant foil to the wheat biscuits to have some fresh orange segments on the side, but it doesn't really work in the cereal itself.

Herbed Baked Beans on Toast
A sprinkling of dried herbs as you as are heating the beans enhances their savouriness.

Pitta Bread Stuffed with Sausage Rice (start the night before)
Cook 150g of rice the night before; you'll want to work with previously cooked rice the next day. In the morning, grill or bake 4 veggie sausages (left over from the second packet of sausages for Day 3's dinner), then cut into thin disks and set aside. Fry 2 chopped cloves of garlic, then add the rice and 2 tablespoons soy sauce. Heat through until hot, then add the sausage discs and cook long enough to warm through. Have some pittas ready in the toaster, then allow the mixture to cool slightly while you are toasting the pitta. Then fill away.

Rolls with Cucumber, Celery and Homemade Caramelised Onion Hummus and Rolls with Peanut Butter and Finely Chopped Celery
Take your 500g bag of chickpeas and put in a large pan of water. Bring to the boil, and boil for 5 minutes, turn off the heat and allow to stand for an hour. Drain, then put the chickpeas in fresh water. Bring to the boil, turn down to a gentler boil and cook for about an hour, until soft. When cool, in one box put 200g (cooked weight) chickpeas. Then put 400g cooked chickpeas in one plastic box and 400g in another (a little more won't hurt – it depends on how much your chickpeas have swelled. They usually double in weight when soaked and cooked, so I am working on this premise, but it does vary a little).
Take one of your 500g cooked chickpeas and blend them with 2 tablespoons tahini, the juice of a lemon, 2 tablespoons walnut oil, 2 cloves of chopped garlic and a little water if necessary. Add salt and pepper to taste. Slice two onions, then fry very slowly for 10 minutes until soft and brown. Mix into the hummus, then pop in the fridge.

In the morning, spread the rolls with the hummus, then add ½ chopped stalk of celery to each roll and some cucumber slices. You will have about half a cucumber and 4 stalks of celery spare (the rest is used in the Bibimbap) .For the peanut butter rolls the next day, mix in two finely chopped stalks of celery with about 2 heaped tablespoons peanut butter before spreading.

Wraps Filled with Chickpeas Smashed with vegan Worcestershire Sauce and Sliced Olives
Take the 200g box of chickpeas from the fridge and roughly mash them with 1 teaspoon Worcestershire Sauce and a few splashes of soy sauce. Take the olives left over from this week's Rice Balls (or as many as you would enjoy), slice them, then mix them in with the smashed chickpeas. Fill your wraps.

Pittas filled with Grated Carrot, Chopped Nuts and Chipotle Cream Cheese
Beat in about ½–1 teaspoon of chipotle paste into the cream cheese before combining with the other ingredients; just enough to give it a little kick!

Wraps Filled with Baby Corn, Peanuts and Tomatoes Splashed with Soy Sauce
Slice the 135g corn into rounds, mix with the peanuts and sliced tomatoes, then lay on flat wraps. Splash with soy sauce then wrap up.

Herby Scones and Chipotle Hummus
For the scones, follow the recipe used for those served alongside the Five Onion Teriyaki Soup in the winter recipes. For the hummus, follow the recipe above (using the remaining box of cooked chickpeas), but instead of the onions, add 1 teaspoon chipotle paste before blending.

Dinners for Autumn, Week Three

1. Roasted Vegetable Satay

2. Textured Split Pea Burgers with Gherkins, Brown Sauce, Garlic Tomatoes and Tomato Ketchup

3. Sunset Mashed Potato over Garlic Wholefood Passata

4. Peasy Dahl with Carrots and Celery

5. Wholewheat Penne with Smoked Almonds, Sweetcorn and Garlic Breadcrumbs

6. Autumn Spiral High Tea: Hot Pizza Rolls, Spiral Spelt Rolls and Allspice Date and Mango Cake with a Mango and Cardamom Sauce

7. Contemporary Stuffed Peppers

Shopping List for Dinners for Autumn, Week Three

	Prices
Vegetables/Fruit	
750g organic onions	00.95
759g organic carrots	00.95
packet of 3 garlic bulbs	00.85
500g organic potatoes	01.15
mixed chillies	00.57
2 x pack 3 mixed peppers at 92p each	01.84
1 large aubergine	00.65
1 lime	00.29
3 x 350g tomatoes at 71p each	02.13
250g chestnut mushrooms	00.95
one head of celery	00.53
4 medium courgettes	001.50
1 large swede	00.50
3 x 350g cherry tomatoes at 58p each	01.74
Fridge	
375g puff pastry	01.00
vegan margarine	01.20
500ml coconut yoghurt	01.20
190g vegan red cheddar	02.20
250 ml oat cream	00.75
100g vegan ham-style slices	01.89
Cupboard	
soy sauce	00.42
1.5kg plain flour	00.45
680g gherkins	00.69
800g wholemeal bread	00.45
130g walnuts	01.29
500g soft brown sugar	00.99

200g bicarbonate of soda	00.69
270g apple sauce	00.49
1 kg long grain rice	00.40
2 x 400g reduced fat coconut milk at 59p each	01.77
340g crunchy peanut butter	00.65
olive oil	01.20
500g yellow split peas	00.55
540g brown sauce	00.28
500g tomato ketchup	00.38
500g wholewheat penne	00.55
125g dried yeast	00.64
1 kg white spelt flour	02.00
1 kg wholemeal spelt flour	02.00
80g sundried tomato paste	00.75
80g ready to eat dried mango (e.g. Urban Fruit)	01.80
250g chopped dates	01.00
37g allspice	01.50
850g mango pulp	01.50
31g whole cardamom pods	01.50
105g Twiglets	01.00
2 x 65g smoked almonds at £1.50 each	03.00
Freezer	
900g frozen sweetcorn	00.89
TOTAL	**£51.67**

Already accounted for: garam masala, baking powder
and mixed herbs.

Roasted Vegetable Satay

Nothing intensifies the sweetness of vegetables more than roasting them, and nothing makes them more comforting that an Indonesian style Gado-Gado sauce.

Ingredients

2 tins reduced fat coconut milk
3 tablespoons crunchy peanut butter
1 tablespoon dark soy sauce
1 large aubergine, cubed
4 courgettes, cut into thin batons
200g cherry tomatoes, halved
250g chestnut mushrooms, quartered
4 tablespoons frozen sweetcorn
2 tablespoons oil
1 lime

Method

1) Preheat oven to Gas Mark 7/ 220°C/425°F.

2) Toss the vegetables in the oil in a shallow baking dish. Level them out with the back of a spoon until you have an even layer, then roast for approximately 20 minutes until all are tender. Cut this way, they should roast evenly.

3) In the meantime, empty the coconut milk into a wok and heat gently, until it is just beginning to bubble, then thoroughly stir in the peanut butter until there are no clumps. Mix in the soy sauce.

4) Simmer very gently until the vegetables are ready. After blotting any excess oil, add the vegetables to the sauce, together with the frozen sweetcorn. Heat through, then serve garnished with a sliced lime; the slices can then be nicked and squeezed over each portion.

Textured Split Pea Burgers with Gherkins, Brown Sauce, Garlic Tomatoes and Ketchup

These burgers are more interesting both to eat and to look at if you keep the split peas whole rather than blending them with the potatoes, to create a textured burger. A 500g packet of split beans costs pennies (about 55p on average), and you can get two meals out of it.

Ingredients

250g yellow split peas from a 500g packet

1 red chilli, chopped fairly finely

200g cherry tomatoes

1 tablespoon olive oil

4 garlic cloves, chopped very finely

2 large cooked potatoes

1 onion, chopped finely

30g vegan margarine

About 1 tablespoon flour for shaping the burgers

Method

1) Thoroughly rinse the split peas (swish them in a colander until the water is no longer cloudy) and discard any stones – they do appear now and then.

2) Boil them for 35–40 minutes, until you can squash one between the thumb and forefinger, but not until they form a puree (keep checking).

3) Set aside to cool while you mash the potato with the marg, then mix in the two cloves of garlic, onion and chilli.

4) When the split peas are cool, mix them into the potato mixture.

5) Flour your hands and shape the mixture into burgers. If you have a burger press, so much the better. They are not expensive (Argos and Lakeland do them for around £6), but if you cannot manage it this week it isn't vital. However, if you enjoy making burgers, a press is worth saving up for).

6) Fry the burgers on both side just to firm and heat them up and retain the pretty yellow colour.

7) In another pan, fry the tomatoes with the rest of the garlic just until they start to wilt.

8) Serve the burgers according to preferences with gherkins, garlic tomatoes, brown sauce and tomato ketchup. All or any are scrumptious accompaniments.

Sunset Mashed Potato over Garlic Wholefood Passata

There are two reasons for this epithet: firstly, some believe that cheese gives you nightmares – (does that apply to vegan cheese?) – so it is best to eat this ingredient at sunset, not too close to bedtime; secondly, the red cheese gives the mashed potato the beautiful orange glow of a setting sun. The fluffy, creamy potatoes and swede and the slightly acidic sweetness of the pureed tomatoes (with their seeds and skin, unlike the bottled passata) are a combination which hits your tongue in lots of delectable ways.

Ingredients

500g old potatoes, such as Maris Piper, peeled and cut into largish, uniform chunks

140g vegan red cheese

2 cloves garlic, chopped finely

400g cherry tomatoes

1 medium swede, cubed

55g vegan margarine

1 tablespoon oil

Method

1)   Preheat the oven to Gas Mark 6/200°C/400°F.

2)   Boil the swede and potatoes (in separate saucepans) until tender (about 20 minutes).

3)   Mash the potato with the cheese and 25g marg. Mash the swede with the remaining 30g marg.

4) Fry the tomatoes with the garlic until they have both softened, then puree in the food processor.

5) In a clear round ovenproof glass dish, layer the swede followed by the tomatoes, then finish with the cheesy potatoes.

6) With the flat of a knife, fan out the potatoes until they resemble a flaming sun.

7) Bake for 20 minutes until orangey golden brown.

Peasy Dahl with Carrots and Celery

This is both easy peasy and reminiscent of pease pudding, but the marg and spices render it luscious rather than austere. It will use the rest of the packet of 500g split peas, but if you don't want to cook this today split peas have a very long shelf life (about 18 months). If you like a more fluid dahl, you could either add more melted marg or stock, depending on your financial situation or health preferences.

Ingredients

250g yellow split peas
4 cloves garlic
1 teaspoon garam masala
4 carrots, chopped

4 stick celery, chopped
2 onions, chopped
85g vegan margarine

Method

1) Pre-boil the carrots for 10 minutes and set aside. Boil the split peas for about 40–45, until they are just starting to go mushy.

2) Melt the margarine (but not until it browns) and gently fry the onions until transparent, then add the garam masala and fry for another few minutes.

3) Add the celery and carrots and fry for another three minutes.

4) Add the garlic and gently fry for two minutes. Start toasting the pitta bread.

5) Combine the garlic with the split peas, stir thoroughly, and serve with toasted pitta bread.

Wholewheat Penne with Smoked Almonds, Sweetcorn and Garlic Breadcrumbs

This is hearty stuff; nutrient-rich sweetcorn, wholewheat pasta, wholewheat breadcrumbs and smoked almonds. This mix of ingredients is as tasty as it is wholesome.

Ingredients

Two slices wholemeal bread, blitzed into breadcrumbs in a food processor.
340g wholewheat pasta
65g smoked almonds

2 cloves garlic, chopped
1 tablespoon olive oil
4 tablespoons frozen sweetcorn, thawed

Method

1) Fry the breadcrumbs in olive oil with garlic until crisp, boiling the water for the pasta as you do so.

2) Boil pasta for about 11 minutes, until al dente.

3) When the pasta is cooked, immediately add the sweetcorn, smoked almonds and breadcrumbs.

4) On a very low light, toss the whole for one minute. This will keep the breadcrumbs crispy without drying out the remaining ingredients.

If you would like to make the Contemporary Stuffed Peppers this week, double and cook the mixture (excepting the pasta and sweetcorn) and refrigerate.

AUTUMN SPIRAL HIGH TEA

Spiral Spelt Rolls, Hot Pizza Rolls and Allspice Date and Mango Cake with a Mango and Cardamom Sauce

This is an autumnal high tea, themed around bonfires and warming foods with earthy and fiery colours.

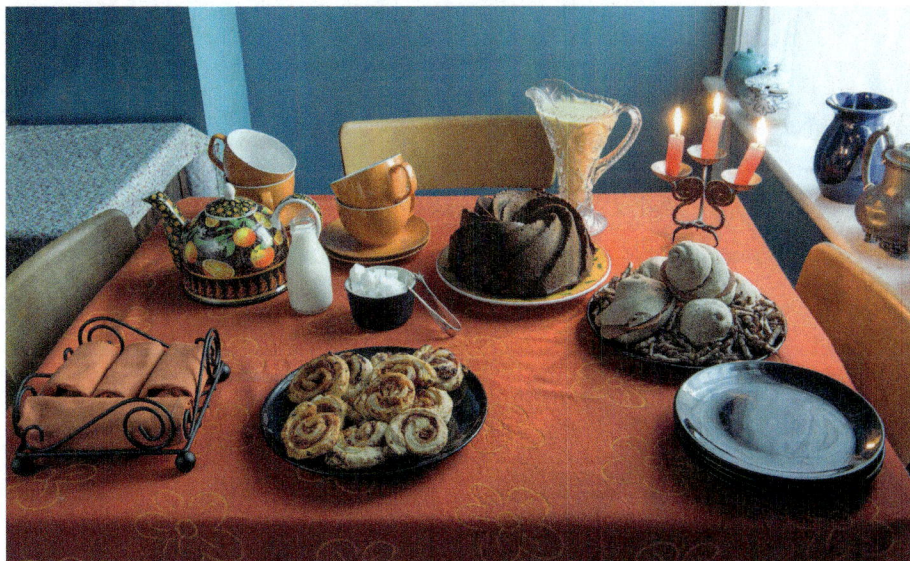

Spiral Spelt Rolls

This will make 16 rolls, two each (i.e. 8) for the Autumn High Tea and two each for the lunch on the same weekend. Freeze the ones you are not using, and remove from the freezer on the morning they are to be eaten. What is so intriguing about this recipe is wondering how the spirals will turn out, because no two are the same. Generally speaking, the skinnier the strips, the more defined the spiral will be, so if you would like a variety of formations for your spirals, make your little balls of dough slightly different sizes. For the Autumn Spiral High Tea, fill the rolls with vegan ham and arrange on a bonfire of Twiglets.

Ingredients

3¼ teaspoons dried yeast
3¼ teaspoons brown sugar
200ml barely warm water
3 teaspoons olive oil

2 teaspoons salt
2 teaspoons dried mixed herbs
337g wholemeal spelt flour
337g plain white spelt flour

Method

1) Put the sugar and yeast into a medium sized bowl then add 200ml of barely warm water (turn on the hot tap — if it hasn't been used recently — and when it is starting to warm up, have your measuring jug ready).

2) Put the bowl somewhere warm, like under a heated radiator, and leave for 15 minutes.

3) In a large bowl, mix the two flours and salt, make a well in the centre, then pour in the liquid yeast mixture. Mix with a wooden spoon, then gradually add roughly 200ml water. You want a slightly wet mixture, because when you knead it, then roll it out later, you will be using more flour.

4) Knead on a floured work surface or board for 10 minutes, stretching it with the heels of your hands, pulling it back and screwing your knuckles into it, so you give it a really thorough pounding.

5) Leave in the same warm place for 2 hours, covered with a clean tea towel; this is why you need a large bowl, because if it is too small, when the dough rises it will stick to the towel and you'll have to peel off all the webby bits. Five minutes before the end, pre-set the oven to 180°C/ 350°F/Gas Mark 4. Grease two baking trays. Put the dough on a floured surface and knead gently for about 2 minutes, then transfer it to a cutting board and shape it into a ball. Cut this into quarters, then eighths, then sixteenths.

6) Form each piece into a little ball. Take the one ball, then roll it with the flats of your two hands into a long round strip, like fat spaghetti, to a length of 30 cm (the length of a ruler).

7) Roll up the strip into a spiral-shaped roll, put on a greased baking tray, and then continue with the others.

8) Bake at 180°C/350°F/Gas Mark 4 for 25 minutes; tap the bottom of the rolls and if they sound hollow, they are done. For the Autumn Spiral High Tea, put four rolls on a bed of Twiglets to resemble a bonfire.

Hot Pizza Rolls

This is one of those recipes that are so easy to customise, and can be as basic or elaborate as your purse and inclinations allow. I wanted one with fiery colours; this is supremely simple, but flavoursome nonetheless, because the sundried tomato paste will do all the flavouring for you.

Ingredients

1 325g pack of ready-rolled puff pastry
1 190g jar sundried tomato paste

1 yellow pepper, chopped
1–2 teaspoon dried mixed herbs (depending on taste)

Method

1) Preheat the oven to 220°C/430°F/Gas Mark 7. Grease a baking tray.

2) Unroll the pastry, then cover it with sundried tomato paste.

3) Sprinkle with herbs, then scatter with the yellow pepper.

4) Roll up, cut into thick slices, then bake on your greased tray for 20–25 minutes.

Allspice Date and Mango Cake with Mango and Cardamom Sauce

If any single ingredient symbolises the beginnings of fusion food in England, it is Allspice. Allspice is ground from a single berry (of the Pimento Dioica tree from Central America), but in the fifteenth century, the British thought it tasted like the combined flavours of cloves, cinnamon and nutmeg, so they called it Allspice. It often turns up in chutneys and pickles, and is especially lovely with date-based preserves, so it is natural choice for this cake.

Ingredients

For the Cake

100g 'ready to eat' dried mango (regular dried mango will be too chewy)

200g chopped dates (not rolled in sugar)

175ml water

280g soft brown sugar

3 tablespoons apple sauce

450g plain flour

1½ teaspoon bicarbonate of soda

2 teaspoons baking powder

1 teaspoon Allspice

pinch of salt

225ml vegan plain yoghurt

100g pecan nuts, broken into quarters (break in two vertically first)

For the Sauce

150ml soya cream (or Elmlea plant double cream if you prefer)

425g tin mango puree

4 cardamom pods, split open

Method

1) Put the dates in the water and bring to the boil. Bring down to a simmer, then cook gently until the dates soften. Beat with a wooden spoon until you have a puree. Leave to cool. Drain the mangos, squeeze dry in a tea towel, then chop finely.

2) Preheat the oven to 180°C/350°F/Gas Mark 4. Grease a silicone Bundt mould (a bit overcautious, but just in case).

3) Cream the margarine and sugar together in a large bowl using an electric hand mixer until you have a light and fluffy mixture.

4) Sift the flour, bicarbonate of soda, baking powder, salt and Allspice into a large bowl.

5) Lightly flour the mango and pecan pieces (otherwise they will sink to the bottom when baked). Alternately, fold in the apple sauce (per tablespoon) and dry ingredients, beginning and ending with the dry ingredients. Stir in the vegan yoghurt, date puree, mangoes and pecans. Spoon into the mould and level off the top.

6) Bake for 50 minutes to an hour. Test the cake by putting a skewer close to the middle.

To make the sauce, simply grind the seeds contained in the split cardamom pods, then whizz them with the plant double cream/ soya cream and mango puree in a food processor until everything is combined and the sauce is slightly thickened. Use the pulse button to avoid over-thickening the cream.

Silicone Bundt moulds are much cheaper than the traditional Bundt tins; this spiral one was bought for £7.99. And you can't beat a self-decoraing cake!

Contemporary Stuffed Peppers (with Sweetcorn Rice)

This is an updated variant on that eighties classic, stuffed peppers, which unfortunately were often dull because of the blandness of the rice used for the stuffing. Thankfully, now we have many more international ingredients from which to choose; you'll enjoy every mouthful of these juicy peppers cradling garlicky crispy filling.

Ingredients

4 peppers, halved and deseeded
2 ends of a wholemeal loaf
25g vegan margarine

200g split peas
35g smoked almonds

Method

1) Cook the split peas in plenty of boiling water for about 30–40 minutes, until tender but not soft.

2) Preheat the oven to 200°C/400°F/Gas Mark 6. Grease a baking tray.

3) Whizz the ends of the loaf in the food processor into breadcrumbs. Fry with margarine and garlic until crisp.

4) Combine the split peas, garlic breadcrumbs and smoked almonds, then fill each pepper half. Put the water on for the rice.

5) Bake for about 15–20 minutes until the peppers are very soft and wrinkly and the filling is slightly browned. (If the latter looks as if it is going to happen too soon before the former, cover the sheet of peppers with loose foil). Cook the rice in the meantime, adding thawed 4 tablespoons sweetcorn a few minutes before the end of the cooking time. Mix when drained.

NB: If you made the wholewheat penne earlier in the week, you could already have the breadcrumbs and almond mixture in the fridge. You could add this with the split peas and the whole will crisp up when you bake the peppers. Otherwise, proceed as below.

Suggestions for Breakfasts and Lunches for Autumn, Week Three

BREAKFASTS

Mustard Mushrooms on Toast

Apricot Porridge

Crumpets with Raspberry Jam

Overnight Oats with Apricots and Coconut Yoghurt

Tomatoes and Spring Onions on Muffins with Walnut Oil

Avocado and Devilled Tomatoes on Toast

Raspberry Oat Thumbprint Bites

LUNCHES

Whole pittas stuffed with Garlic Rice, Cress and Chopped Vegan Ham

Wraps with Apricot, Peanut and Celery Salad in Walnut Oil Dressing

Rolls with Moroccan Hummus and Chopped Celery

Peanut butter and Worcestershire Sauced Tomato Sandwiches

Wraps stuffed with Soy Sweetcorn, Tomatoes and Kidney Beans

Spiral Rolls with Scrambled Tofu

Catherine Wheels

Shopping List for Breakfasts and Lunches
for Autumn, Week Three

Box of cress	00 .24
6 whole-wheat pitta breads	00 .42
200g Moroccan hummus	00 .85
Dijon mustard	00 .47
400g closed cup white mushrooms	01.05
500g dried apricots	02.29
2 x pack of 6 tomatoes	01.18
4 toasting muffins	00.39
2 avocados	01.49
454g raspberry jam	00.65
6 crumpets	00.35
Bunch of spring onions	00.45
2 x 400g tin kidney beans at 30p each	00.60
349g tofu	01.25
8 wraps	00.89
800g whole-wheat bread	00.50
TOTAL	**£13.07**
DINNERS	**£51.67**
TOTAL WITH DINNERS	**£64.74**

Already accounted for: sweetcorn, spiral rolls, catherine wheels, rice, celery, sweetcorn, peanut butter Worcestershire sauce, walnut oil, coconut yoghurt, ham, soft brown sugar, apple sauce, paprika, cumin and vegan marg.

Notes on Breakfasts and Lunches for Autumn, Week Three

Mustard Mushrooms on Toast
Clean the mushrooms, slice them, then lightly fry in a non-stick pan with 2 teaspoons each of vegan marg and Dijon mustard plus 2 chopped garlic cloves. Pile onto toast.

Apricot Porridge (start the night before)
Soak 16 dried apricots in plenty of water overnight. In the morning, drain and pat dry, then add half of them to your cooked porridge. Keep the rest in a sealed container until tomorrow.

Overnight Oats with Apricot and Yoghurt (start the night before)
There will be 275g yoghurt remaining from the Allspice Date and Mango Cake. Mix this with your reserved apricots (see above – it will be 8 previously soaked dried apricots) and your oats overnight to be ready in the morning.

Tomatoes and Spring Onions on Muffins with Walnut Oil
Lightly fry two chopped spring onions with three tomatoes in a little walnut oil until the onions are tender but still firm, then pile onto toasted muffins.

Avocado and Devilled Tomatoes on Toast
Mash 2 avocados, then stir in 3 chopped tomatoes. Splash with vegan Worcestershire sauce and sprinkle with black pepper, then pile onto toast.

Raspberry Oat Thumbprint Bites
Grease a baking sheet and turn the oven on to 180°C/350°F/Gas Mark 4. Take 8 tablespoons porridge oats and pulverise them in the food processor until you have oat 'flour'. Cream 2 tablespoons vegan marg with 2 tablespoons soft brown sugar. Add 2 teaspoons apple sauce and mix until well combined. Gradually add the oat flour and stir gently until thorough mixed (reserve a little to flour your hands). Make ping-pong sized biscuits by breaking off small pieces with your floured hands, then rolling into spheres. Put these spheres on your greased baking tray, allowing room for spreading. In each biscuit, make a well with your thumb, then fill this well with raspberry jam. Cook for 10 minutes, or until golden. Take care – the jam will be burning hot!

Whole Pittas Stuffed with Garlic Rice, Cress and Chopped Vegan Ham (start the night before)

Cook the 200g rice remaining to you the night before. In the morning, reheat by frying wit 2 chopped cloves of garlic. Chop 4 slices of vegan ham (you'll be using the rest for the High Tea), mix with the rice, stir in the cress and stuff your pittas.

Peanut Butter and Worcestershire Sauced Tomato Sandwiches

Spread your sandwiches with peanut butter and add tomato slices (from 3 medium tomatoes). Sprinkle with vegan Worcestershire Sauce.

Wraps Stuffed with Soy Sweetcorn, Tomatoes and Kidney Beans

Spread out 4 tablespoons frozen sweetcorn on the plate to thaw. Slice 3 tomatoes thinly and strain two tins of kidney beans. Toss the defrosted sweetcorn in a bowl with a tablespoon of soy sauce, then mix with the kidney beans.

Lay the wraps flat, then spread with the kidney beans and sweetcorn. Lay tomato slices on the top of each filled wrap, then fold in the sides, top and bottom.

Spiral Rolls with Spiced Scrambled Tofu

The rolls come from the batch baked for the High Tea. To make scrambled tofu, break it up and fry it with a splash of soy sauce, two chopped spring onions and a pinch of paprika and cumin.

Catherine Wheels

From the High Tea batch.

Printed in Great Britain
by Amazon